FROM THE CHIEF

FRANK COMMENTARY

ON CURRENT

LAW ENFORCEMENT ISSUES

BY

JERRY BOYD, M.S.

CHIEF OF POLICE, RETIRED

DEDICATION

This book is dedicated to every law enforcement officer in the United States, at every level of government, who remains true to his or her oath of office. That is easy to do at times but in the current political environment in which we find ourselves it can be extremely difficult. Those who adhere to their oath to protect, serve, and uphold the Constitution of the United States are particularly deserving of our thanks.

ACKNOWLEDGMENTS

Though this book is brief, no book can be written without inspiration and support. Good leadership has always been important to me in my career and in life. At the outset of my career, with the Los Angeles County Sheriff's Department, I worked one of the most violent crime rate areas in the nation. I was privileged to work for a Patrol Station Commander at Firestone Station, Captain M. Dean Wert, whose example has served me well for nearly fifty years.

From the Chief was a regular column which appeared monthly in **AmericanCop** magazine. I wish to thank the Publisher, Roy Huntington and the Editor, Suzi Huntington, for their foresight in seeing the need for such a column, and for their support over the years the column was featured before the magazine ceased publication.

My wife, Jay, has been a supporter of my efforts, and chief proofreader, I might add, for over twenty years. Thanks!

ABOUT THE AUTHOR

The author lives in Eastern Oregon and is currently in his 50th year in public safety. He currently serves as the Reserve Commander with a local law enforcement agency and coordinates a five county, regional law enforcement training academy. Beginning his career at age 18 he served as a Technical Reserve (Communications) with the Los Angeles County Sheriff's Department. After his twenty-first birthday he became a regular Deputy and served briefly as a Deputy at Men's Central Jail prior to beginning the academy.

Graduating as the honor cadet in his class Jerry was transferred, upon graduation, to patrol at the Sheriff's Firestone Station. That patrol station served the second most violent crime rate area in the United States. After three years at Firestone, as a patrol Deputy, Field Training Officer, and Acting Sergeant he transferred to Headquarters Detective Division-Metropolitan Bureau where he served for one year prior to promotion to Sergeant. As a Sergeant he worked Patrol at the Norwalk, Firestone, and Carson stations and received SWAT training from the Sheriff's Special Enforcement Bureau.

In 1975 he joined the newly formed Irvine, California Police Department where he served as a Lieutenant for three years. Upon his promotion to Captain he was assigned to command the department's Operation's Division. In 1981 he was appointed Chief of Police for the City of Coronado California and served in that capacity for ten years. The last five years of his full time law enforcement career were spent as Chief of Police in Martinez, California.

Following retirement Jerry was appointed to serve as Mutual Aid Communication Officer for the Inland Region (20 counties) of the California Governor's Office of Emergency Services. He served in that capacity for six years and at the same time was Chief of a volunteer Fire/Rescue Department in Shasta County California.

In 2003 Jerry and his family re-located to Eastern Oregon and not long after he was appointed Director of a Consolidated 9-1-1 Dispatch Center, a position he held for eight and one half years until again retiring.

Jerry and his wife, Jay, live on a small ranch in Eastern Oregon where they have raised border collies and American Paint Horses. In addition to riding his horses, he follows a consistent workout program, and he and his wife hike in the local mountains.

Jerry has a Master of Science degree in Criminal Justice Administration from California State University at Long Beach. He is the author of *Firestone Park: Policing South Central Los Angeles*, available at Amazon.com.

FOREWORD

During the years *AmericanCop* magazine was published one of its most read and most popular monthly columns was ***From The Chief***. That column was written by retired Chief of Police Jerry Boyd and it generated more positive Letters to the Editor than nearly all other columns in the magazine combined.

Jerry has spent fifty years in public safety, the majority as a law enforcement officer. He served as a Police Chief for fifteen years, a Fire Chief for four years and a 9-1-1 Center Director for eight and a half years. He has always credited his leadership style and perspective to the guidance of God and the excellent mentoring he received during his early years in our profession as a member of the Los Angeles County Sheriff's Department. His time with that agency as a Deputy and Sergeant was in the turbulent sixties and seventies and was served in one of the most violent crime rate areas in the United States. Strict adherence to the oath of office and professional standards was critical and charted the course he would later follow as a police chief.

I believe Jerry's writing resonates powerfully with our fellow law enforcement professionals for a number of reasons. Jerry is firmly guided by strong principles that he adheres to despite current trends. He has never lost sight of what it means to work the street. He places the well-being of those he leads and the communities he has served well above himself and he doesn't bow to politics. In short, Jerry is the leader every good cop in America wants because he has your back when you are doing the right thing whether others like it or not. When you read Jerry's writing, the heart, wisdom and character of the man shines through.

This book contains all of his columns published in *AmericanCop* as well as others written since the magazine ceased publication. Readers, depending upon their perspective, may or may not agree with Jerry's point of view on every subject addressed. If, however, his writings motivate thoughtful reflection on critical issues which challenge us today they will have served their purpose.

It is my privilege to recommend this book to you and it is truly my blessing to work with Jerry as he continues his selfless involvement in law enforcement in a Reserve capacity.

Brian Harvey
Chief of Police
La Grande, Oregon

INTRODUCTION

Shortly after *American Cop™* magazine began publication a few years ago I was asked by the Editor to consider writing a quarterly column which discussed pertinent law enforcement issues of the day from the perspective of a department head. *From the Chief* was the title of that column and it graced every issue, at first quarterly and then monthly, until the magazine ceased publication in August 2014.

Reader feedback was crucial to the column with subject matter focusing on issues raised by, or topics suggested by readers. Feedback was generally positive though not universally so. My perspective was and is that of a twenty-seven year department head in public safety with fifteen of those years as a Chief of Police. I am opinionated, particularly when it comes to peace officers adhering to their Code of Ethics and I am adamant that "political correctness" has no place in the chief's office. "PC" is destructive of an agency's morale and is detrimental to the good of the communities we serve.

This book is a compilation of all of the **From the Chief** columns printed in *American Cop* and are included with permission. I appreciate their permission to use those columns. In addition there are other articles which either were submitted for publication prior to the demise of the magazine or which I have written since then.

While some readers of this little book may not agree with my position on some issues, I hope that these writings at least generate some thought about the important subjects they address. As I suspect most readers of this work will be law enforcement professionals please be safe out there and always, always adhere to your Oath of Office.

Jerry Boyd
Baker City, Oregon
November 2014

TABLE OF CONTENTS

Cops and the Current Administration

I'll state two things up front. One: I know this will not be well-accepted by all who read it. Two: I have not written this without considerable thought, nor is it based upon partisan politics. I've always cast my vote for the one I believe to be most qualified for a particular office without regard to that person's political party affiliation. Having said that, I don't believe any ethical professional law enforcement officer can in good conscience support the current administration of this nation.

As law enforcement officers we take an oath to uphold the Constitution of the United States and to enforce the law without prejudice. There are too many examples in which the facts make it clear the current administration, which should be held to a standard at least as high as us cops, has failed both to uphold the Constitution and to enforce existing laws. It's almost inconceivable to me how those of us who've sworn to uphold certain standards can possibly support so-called leaders who've failed to do the same.

If the administration's bias against law enforcement without making any effort to determine the facts was ever questioned, it's only necessary to look at the Harvard professor vs. Cambridge, Mass. police sergeant incident and the reaction of the President, for an example. If you question my assertion this administration fails to uphold the law of the land, and, in some cases, blatantly violates those laws, look to the following.

In Your Face Proof

BATF's "Operation Gunrunner" (aka "Fast and Furious") clearly violated existing federal law regarding firearms sales. In this misguided, politically motivated operation the lives of many were, and still are, placed in jeopardy. As a result of this boondoggle, guns illegally trafficked into Mexico were used in the killing of a US federal law enforcement officer. Responsibility for this operation rests not with just one department of the federal government, but with the administration itself.

Clear and indisputable videotaped evidence showed voter intimidation (a violation of federal law) by a group of armed thugs. The "Justice Department" declined to prosecute in spite of clear evidence, and did so for blatantly political reasons. Decisions by the Attorney General directly reflect upon the administration, which he's a part of.

Current federal law makes illegal entry into the US a crime. Illegal immigrants can be prosecuted for that crime or, at the very least, are to be deported. Congress has refused to pass the "Dream Act," which was introduced to grant amnesty to many who are here illegally. The administration, in violation of the Constitution and in direct opposition to the separation of powers clause, has chosen to ignore the decision of Congress and promote "backdoor amnesty" by restricting deportation of illegals to only those with a criminal record.

Supporting Evil Through Selfishness

If you accept my premise that no cop in good conscience can support, through their vote or their financial contributions, a regime engaging in such practices, you might wonder why some cops do exactly that. I think it's because many LEOs are unionized and this administration, if nothing else, has maintained cozy relationships with unions since day one. Cops who put their own financial well being above their duty and their oath of office support unethical and, in some cases, questionably illegal actions by elected officials.

Now more than ever before in our nation's history, we in law enforcement have a major decision to make. Are we going to allow ourselves to be manipulated and used politically because we think by doing so we'll benefit financially? Or are we going to stand on the principles that in the past have set our profession apart, in a positive way, from those whose only interest is drinking from the public trough?

It galls me to see men and women in uniform standing behind this President during one of his numerous public appearances, believing as I do they're being used by one who really does not support the law enforcement mission. It's one thing to be assigned to a presidential protection detail; it's a legitimate and necessary activity. But to allow ourselves to be put on display by one who's the classic Machiavellian politician is quite another.

Maybe we ought to rethink the question of whether supporting an administration, which has little respect for the rule of law, is really in our best interests, or, more importantly, the right thing to do.

Killing Your Agency with Suck-ups?

Some things never change — or maybe they do. Let's talk about promotions, and for those so inclined to promote, how to go about it the right way. The promotional process can vary by agency and by the rank aspired. There probably is not a "typical" path or process to follow for those seeking higher rank. There is, however, one component of sewing on the stripes or pinning on the bar, which is relatively common and that's the promotability of the candidate. How is it determined? Depending on the department, it may involve a review of past performance evaluations or command personnel actually ranking applicants based upon their impressions and opinions as to how the aspirant would perform if selected for the position.

While I believe the assessment of the promotability component is valid and important, it's all too often an invitation for inappropriate behavior on the part of candidates. Knowing that at least a part of the process could involve subjective or even favorite treatment, some (thankfully not all) applicants engage in behavior which is detrimental to the organization and, in particular, morale and good working relationships. In blunt terms, some candidates in order to gain favor with their superiors engage in a whole lot more butt kissing than productive work. They go to extremes to make good impressions, take credit for the work of others, and will throw coworkers under the bus in a heartbeat.

Unprincipled Peter

Frankly, any candidate for any rank who plays politics, kisses butt, puts down others or is more show than go doesn't deserve promotional consideration. If below-the-belt tactics prove successful and if, indeed, they are promoted it's a clear invitation for the Peter Principle to manifest itself. "Success by suck up" is guaranteed to result in a deterioration of morale as good, hard working, fair playing competitors see little benefit in doing it the right way.

We've all seen it. The guy or gal whose work is designed to impress rather than to serve; the "it's all about me" showboat who has no concept of what teamwork is and no desire to be a teammate; the one who will never offer constructive criticism even when it's invited, but is always first to be a "yes man" even when yes is the wrong answer.

Who's to blame for the successes some suckups seem to enjoy? Those above them in rank who let such cops get away with it, who never call them on it, and who let their egos be flattered by the insincere attention suckups pay to anyone they think can help their career aspirations.

Being The Best

Don't get me wrong, there's a legitimate place for ambitious, play-by-the-rules cops to seek out mentors. The seeking, though, should be for the purpose of learning — not for gaining favor. I've had some outstanding mentors throughout my career. Some I sought out and some on their own initiative took me under their wing, probably to keep me from making a big mistake.

The mentoring I was fortunate to receive was never offered for any purpose other than making me the best I could be, at whatever rank I might have held at the moment. There was not nor should there have been, any link to any present or future promotional process.

Good cops are good judges of human nature, and are very adept at distinguishing the real from the phony. As a chief, I've always thought my role in selecting those to be promoted involved choosing only those with legitimate credentials. For any top cop to select a suckup for promotion above those who are the real meal deal is to do the organization a huge disservice. For anyone in the command structure to allow the phony ladder-climber any measure of success at all is to stab the organization in the back.

So, for those seeking to promote who want to have a sense of pride rather than shame if the promotional effort is successful, take this bit of advice from an old timer. Work hard, study hard, find good role models and mentors, and let your actions — not your mouth — speak for you. If you work for a good organization, that approach (not the butt kissing approach) will serve you well. If you're successful in achieving the rank to which you aspire, you'll have the respect of those you lead. And, there's no better feeling than that.

The Yes-Man: No Thank You

There's a phenomenon running rampant in society and in our profession today; it's the tendency for those in positions of responsibility to be yes-men when it comes to giving advice and feedback to the boss. In law enforcement, no one should be a yes-man. We took an oath and that alone should make it clear we're required to be truthful, not "politically correct."

While every cop has the duty to provide honest and accurate feedback up the chain of command, that responsibility clearly exists at the supervisory, mid management, and management level. Yet too many examples exist, some of which make the news, where the people with responsibility are abandoning their duty just to "make the boss happy."

As a chief, I don't want or need yes-men. If that's all you're capable of or have the guts to be, you're of no benefit to me — or the organization. I don't have all the answers and I want staff I can rely on to "tell it like it is" … tactfully and in as positive a manner as possible? Absolutely. But you do the department, community and me a disservice when you withhold your best professional judgment and soundest advice. If all I wanted, and the department needed was someone to tell me what I already know or believe, we could save a lot of salaries.

Cesspool of Mediocrity

For years now, I've been observing this yes-man trend grow to the point where far too many agencies are afflicted with it. I've often wondered why this is occurring, and even asked those I've seen engaging in this behavior why they do it. The answers point squarely to the "it's all about me" syndrome, which appears to have rapidly replaced the "department comes first" mentality.

I have seen, and even worked for, some law enforcement agencies, which were once considered within the profession to be among the very best. Today some of those agencies have sunk deeply into mediocrity with several now residing in the cesspool of being under DOJ investigations. The pity is such downfalls were unnecessary and very preventable.

Those I've asked point blank why they don't tell the boss what needs to be heard rather than what they think the boss wants to hear generally have similar answers. They range from, "I don't want to make him angry" to, "he'll hold it against me" and, "hey, I want to get promoted." Well, the cold hard truth is this: Any boss who gets angry when one of his trusted officers of any rank tactfully and respectfully gives input not 100-percent in line with his, is not a very good boss to begin with. The fact is any boss who holds such input against a subordinate is probably not the boss you want to work for — if you are a professional.

If holding back important and honest input prevents you from being promoted, don't you wonder if the promotion would be worth it? Or, if you are promoted, will the pressures on you to keep the truth inside become even more severe? If you're someone with ethics and integrity, I can assure you that will eat at your insides big time.

Speak Your Mind

Ask this question as well: What are the pitfalls attendant to being nothing more than a yes-man? I can think of many. One is the organization stagnates, or worse, illegal or unprofessional practices creep into the agency because no one had the guts to let the boss know what was really happening.

I know from experience there are different kinds of chiefs and sheriffs. Some actually still remember what it was like on the streets. Some (the better ones in my view) still hit the streets often enough to stay connected with the real world. And some actually take the time to seek input from those impacted by decisions made at the top. Others ride a desk and get so involved in things exterior to the department, like political posturing, that they have little understanding of what the reality is within the organization. In the case of this sort of "top cop," yes-men only make the problem worse.

I know of one nameless department, which, at the moment, is in serious trouble with its constituents and the federal government, having had numerous investigations launched against it. The top guy is feeling a lot of heat. Knowing what I do about him and the agency, much of it is well deserved. The cause? A whole bunch of management folks who've been yes-men for years. His reaction is to throw all of those yes-men under the bus, loudly proclaiming for all to hear, "they never told me."

Is this the reward you want for being a yes-man? Do you really want the public blaming you for your silence? And what do you think of your promotional chances now? So from an old chief who's seen the serious downsides of yes-manism — man up. Do what you're paid to do, not what you think will feather your nest. In the long run, it won't.

Poor Leadership: Killing Our Profession

Interestingly, since the first of my columns appeared, every single topic I have addressed has resulted from reader suggestions or requests. Does everyone agree with my perspective? Of course not, and they shouldn't. There's room in every profession for differing opinions and constructive disagreement. Just this past month, a reader asked why I seem to be so opposed to much of what I see in law enforcement today. He went so far as to suggest I might be one of those Neanderthals I detested so much earlier in my career.

In reality, I'm not opposed to much of what I see in law enforcement today. I recently had the opportunity to teach several classes at an academy, attended by those just beginning their journey in the profession. I found their intelligence, enthusiasm, desire and motivation to be everything one could hope for in a professional cop. I deal with young, relatively new law enforcement officers on a daily basis. I find them to be every bit as good, if not better, at what they do than many of my generation who worked the streets ages ago.

Clearly, there's much to like with the tools and technology commonplace in police work in 2012. In short, most of what I see, I like. There is, however, a serious shortcoming in our profession, and it's not one restricted to just a few agencies. That shortcoming, in my view, is leadership. And, if leadership in law enforcement leaves a lot to be desired, as I think it does, it doesn't bode well for the future.

What's Missing?

The thing missing, to put it bluntly: credibility. An absence of credibility results from several related shortcomings. First is a lack of honesty, and second of real-world experience, with an overabundance of what I call "textbook." There's also more focus on too many leaders advancing their personal agendas, rather than helping the troops advance their skill levels. And finally, I see a serious disconnect between the world in which the leader operates and the world the men and women on the street function in.

The lack of honesty is born of political correctness. Let's say your agency has its budget slashed; you and everyone you work with know as a result officer safety will be jeopardized, response times increased and enforcement levels will drop. What does the boss say to the public? "We will continue to provide the appropriate level of service." Hogwash!

I have nothing against college degrees. I have a master's degree in Criminal Justice Administration, myself. But any police leader, whose credentials are mostly academic, without a sufficient dose of street experience to balance out what the ivory tower thinkers preach in the classroom, will be ineffective — and too many today are just that. Publisher, Roy Huntington, covered this very topic in his From the Publisher column (Nov/Dec 2011). As a retired cop, he noticed it too. He said, "It's easy to get so focused on an educational goal — you lose contact with reality." And he's right.

The disconnect between one who rides a desk and one who drives a patrol car is becoming much more common. There was a day in our history when the top cop would roll up his sleeves, hit the streets and get his shoes dirty. It was because workload demanded it, he thought it set a positive example, or he actually still had some cop left in him. That seldom occurs today, except on very small agencies, where the chief often continues to work the field, and is an integral part of the team.

Too many bosses today live in a world of politics, appeasement and advancing agendas, which may or may not have much to do with police work. The troops, on the other hand, keep on doing the heavy lifting. And it seems more often than not, they do it for a leader who neither understands nor appreciates what goes on in a dark alley at 0200 hours.

The Future

To the extent what I say is true, will, over time, have a detrimental effect on our profession. In agencies with a long history of poor leadership we see the results already. Agencies led by inadequate leaders do not retain the best officers — they leave and go elsewhere. Agencies with inadequate leadership stagnate. Organizations with poor leadership can become corrupt. I know of one agency in particular having its own in-house gangs, whose members are nearly as predatory as the Crips, Bloods or MS 13. True story, and I'm not exaggerating! You only have to look at the news to read of out-of-control special units, who eventually get indicted for wholesale criminal acts. That can only occur if there is poor — or no — leadership.

The reality today in many agencies is, in fact, the best leadership often comes at the lowest levels in the organization. The street cops, or at best, first line supervisors, have the experience and integrity all too often lacking at the top. That explains, at least in part, why American COP holds the working street cop in high esteem, and demands — even expects — leaders to rise to the occasion to support these officers. The working cop's level is, indeed, where the future rests.

Who Pays for PTSD?

A reader asked me to comment on the Albuquerque, N.M. Police Association's (APA) practice of giving sums of cash to officers involved in shootings or other traumatic incidents. These payments, averaging several hundred dollars each, are given almost immediately after the incident involving an officer. The media has seized on this practice labeling it a "bounty" system. The union argues such payments are solely intended to assist the officers with expenses incurred as a result of on-duty shootings. What's my take on this?

Over the past few decades, we've learned that although the use of deadly force is something every officer potentially faces, not all officers react in the same manner to such incidents. Some suffer from what the mental health profession has identified as Post Traumatic Stress Disorder (PTSD). It's a factor common to both law enforcement and the military. The highly publicized case of an Army Sergeant murdering 17 Afghan civilians in an unprovoked attack has been attributed to PTSD and serves as an example.

Agency Obligations

Clearly law enforcement agencies have a responsibility to their officers who have been involved not only in deadly force incidents, but in any very traumatic incident which could result in short- or long-term ill effects. The officer's wellbeing, his or her family's, as well as the safety of the public depends upon agencies meeting that responsibility.

It is a common practice for most, but not all, agencies to place officers involved in traumatic incidents on administrative leave to give them an opportunity to decompress. Many agencies offer, and some require counseling for such officers and many require a psychological reevaluation prior to a return to duty. The question in my mind is not whether the costs of such interventions should be on the shoulder of someone other than the officer, but rather whose shoulder.

Professional policing agencies should recognize it's their responsibility to bear the cost of a temporary relief from duty, counseling, and a reevaluation of fitness if it appears such a reevaluation is prudent. While agencies cannot dictate or control what police associations or unions do, it should be possible for the agency and the union to agree on a policy; and one, which minimizes public criticism of both the agency and the police association.

Inviting Criticism?

If the agency has a written protocol for dealing with such incidents, and it should, that policy is open to public review. The agency also has the ability to explain, pre-incident, why the policy is in place and what positive goals it is designed to accomplish. If a non-government entity, such as a police association or union, implements a practice such as the one in Albuquerque it will inevitably give rise to the generally anti-police media misrepresenting it. The usual spin is never designed to make the agency or union look like anything other than bloodthirsty oppressors of the public.

So, no matter how will-intended the APA cash allotment program is, it gives rise to unnecessary suspicion and it duplicates or substitutes for what should be the responsibility of the police department. Doing the right thing must be law enforcement's number one priority. Doing it in a way that minimizes the chance for public criticism must rank high on the priority list as well.

Border Violence Intensifies

Those of us who've worked in jurisdictions adjacent to our nation's border with Mexico are not nearly as shocked as most people at the escalating drug cartel-related violence, which has spilled onto US soil in recent months. Actually, that sort of thing has been occurring for a number of years with little public notice — until now. Several recent incidents of cartel "paybacks," in the form of mass murders in remote areas of Arizona and New Mexico, have led to people asking how such a thing could happen.

Don't beheadings and body burnings happen just south of the border? Well, no, they do happen here too. Get used to it because such incidents will become much more common. And, in the near future, they won't just be restricted to rural areas. Good cops who are in the know predict such mass murders in the larger cities of California, Arizona, New Mexico and Texas are only a matter of time. Despite the assertions of the current administration that "our border has never been safer," the facts prove otherwise.

Handcuffing Ourselves

There are some enlightened and responsible law enforcement leaders — most notably the "Border Sheriffs" — who've seen this coming and have taken reasonable steps to prevent such occurrences. For every one of them, however, there are multiple politically correct police chiefs and sheriffs whose heads are in the sand. They are in denial, and so mired in political correctness not only do they fail to take appropriate enforcement measures, but they also fail to see the problem in the first place.

Federal resources are being constrained by totally unreasonable "rules of engagement," and failure to devote adequate resources in those areas where the problem is most evident merely compound the problem. Worse yet, the so-called Department of Justice, in furtherance of a political agenda, has become an adversary to the very law enforcement agencies with which they should be cooperative partners.

Drug-related violence is bad enough in its own right. Left unchecked, the cartels will continue their efforts to buy off and intimidate government officials on our side of the border, in order to broaden their operational base. Corruption of some elected and appointed officials in the US is inevitable, as they're just as enticed by the prospect of wealth — regardless of the source — as the cartels are. But the problem doesn't end there; that problem alone is serious enough to forever alter the integrity of American law enforcement … I take that back, the potential problem is even more serious.

They Hate Us!

The cartels have no love for the US, and view it only as a rich customer for the goods they have to offer. The cartels are motivated by greed, pure and simple. With the lack of reverence for human life they've demonstrated, nothing and no one will stand in the way of them maximizing financial gain. Thus, it should come as no surprise — except to an administration who is in denial — intelligence information from reliable, non-political sources points to an increasing alliance between cartels and international terrorist organizations. Their number one objective is infliction of death and destruction on US soil and its citizens.

How does this alliance manifest itself? Good sources suggest the following: cartels want weapons, and terrorist organizations have them. Terrorist organizations trade weapons with cartels in exchange for using the cartels' established smuggling routes and tactics to move armed, international terrorists into the US without being detected. Think I'm making this up? Our government has acknowledged one major US-hating terrorist group (Hezbollah) has established enclaves and training camps in Mexico. They are teaching and equipping cartel operatives to further enhance their capability for both violence and intimidation of elected officials. The "quid pro quo"? The cartels, according to actionable intelligence, have moved and are continuing to move Hezbollah operatives closer to, and in some cases across, our international border.

I don't know about the rest of you, but this scenario bothers me a great deal. Most troubling to me: all of this is possible only because of a complacent — and in some cases complicit — law enforcement community. In days past, our profession in this country almost universally had the wisdom, integrity and ethics needed to combat such an obvious threat to our national security. Currently, those characteristics are tragically far from universal, and, all too often, seem to be the exception rather than the rule.

Play – Or Pay

Some months back, I authored a column entitled "Cops and the Current Administration" (Jan/Feb 2012). It suggested supporting an administration, which frequently acts in a manner inconsistent with the US Constitution, is not in our profession's best interests. I received a substantial amount of reader feedback … but no one argued my point. In fact, some of you claimed I should've been more forceful in my criticism. I believe in calling it as I see it, but only when my views are supported by verifiable facts.

There are some recent developments which clearly suggest, at least to me, the philosophy of the administration in power at the moment is to reward those who play ball with its politically correct agenda and to make those who fail to do so pay a price. Given the President's pattern and practice of condemning law enforcement in situations where deadly force has to be used against certain minorities, it's not inappropriate to conclude he is not a particular fan of men and women in blue — most radicals aren't.

I don't think it's a misplaced criticism to suggest the administration, as perhaps best exemplified by the attitudes of DOJ and Homeland Security, really only tolerates law enforcement to the extent it furthers their greater agenda. When law enforcement has the gall to buck the liberal tide, the administration, in sometimes not so subtle ways, does its best to make life miserable for us. Let me provide several examples.

Not Fooling Anyone

Love him or hate him, Maricopa County, Ariz. Sheriff, Joe Arpaio, has not played ball with the administration on the subject of border security, and the impact of illegal alien criminal behavior in his jurisdiction. The payback? The Maricopa Sheriff is subjected to DOJ investigations on multiple fronts.

Meanwhile, ample evidence suggests a DOJ investigation is warranted of the Los Angeles County Sheriff's Department on issues ranging from allegations of prisoner abuse, corruption, granting of promotions for political support of command staff, and bidding irregularities relative to LASD aircraft. Allegations only, but sufficient in volume, scope and seriousness, and were it not for the politically correct ball playing by the LA County Sheriff, Leroy Baca, a DOJ investigation would be almost certain.

Across this nation there's an effort, primarily by elected officials who share the President's political philosophy, to negate the constitutional power and authority of the Office of Sheriff. There is no law enforcement official in our system with greater independence than our elected sheriffs. If one wants to control them, and what aspect of our government does this administration not want to control, the best way to accomplish that is to strip them of their authority. That is precisely what, in the state of Delaware and elsewhere, the political hacks of this administration are attempting to do.

Modern Day Robin Hood?

It's no secret — control over as much as possible is what this regime is all about — and is particularly true when it comes to the environment. For those who've been paying attention, we bought into the bogus global warming garbage spewed by the UN. One of the effects of falling for it, at least in the western states, has been massive closures of national forests to public access. In addition, millions of acres have been decreed to now be wildlands (Goggle: Wildlands Project), and again, are closed to the public — the very public who owns the land.

What does this have to do with law enforcement? It's simple; federal law enforcement agents must enforce such closures. Until recently, such agents lacked authority to enforce state and local laws unless they were appointed by the local sheriff to do so. Many of our western sheriffs, seeing the closure of public lands for what it is rather than what it's purported to be, have refused to give federal agents such as Forest Service LEOs authority within their counties. The administration's response through its minions at the state level? Emasculate the sheriffs by taking away their authority. It's play or pay — the Chicago way of doing things, which Obama was brought up on and clearly favors.

Getting Furious Fast

The DOJ, who should be above reproach, is suspected of violating criminal statutes in the much-discussed "Fast and Furious" gunrunning debacle. For months congress has been investigating just who within DOJ gave the stamp of approval to this enforcement program. Rather than provide the documents subpoenaed by Congress, Attorney General Eric Holder has refused to comply, leaving them no choice but to hold "Contempt of Congress" deliberations.

And while the Obama administration demands cooperation from state, county and local entities, it refuses to cooperate when it is under investigation! President Obama even tried to shield Holder from the very real (and warranted) prospect of criminal prosecution by asserting executive privilege — the same privilege he chided his predecessors for using "when trying to hide behind executive privilege, every time there's something a little shaky that's taking place."

We were promised "the most transparent administration in our nation's history." Really? It's clear to me in the administration's mind there's one set of rules for it and an entirely different set of rules for everyone else.

I'm aware of at least one study underway which is attempting to determine just how much quid pro quo there is in the federal government today. That is, just what is the correlation between supporting the current administration through such things as not towing cars owned by illegal aliens (politically correct LAPD) and the receipt of federal grants? On the flip side, what's the correlation between opposing the administration and being excluded from grant consideration? I have my suspicions, and will be watching closely for the results of the study.

We Can't Do This Alone

Recently (Return Fire, "A Man Of Faith" July 2012) a deputy sheriff from Ohio asked the editor to consider doing an article on faith and law enforcement. Suzi, understandably, explained to do so would be virtually impossible without offending some readers. I'd like to approach the issue from a slightly different angle in hopes it not only is supportive of the deputy, but all readers regardless of whether they're men and women of faith or not.

One thing that's become very clear to me over my years in and around the law enforcement profession is those who try to do this job without some sort of support system (sometimes affectionately referred to as the John Wayne syndrome) are doomed to either failure or personal disaster. Yet, many of us make the mistake of doing precisely that — thinking we're one tough hombre — and other than the backup needed on particular types of calls don't, need help from anyone. Those who push this approach to the extreme too often wind up as alcoholics, divorced, in trouble with Internal Affairs or all of the above.

Cop work is one of the most demanding endeavors you can find short of doing battle as a ground troop in a place like Afghanistan. What we're exposed to throughout a career as we go from call to call ranges from boring to life threatening and everything in between. Any cop who tells me he's never found a call to be gut wrenching or emotional either has no experience or is in a state of denial. I'll never forget the first call that punched me in the gut as a new deputy sheriff. Twins had been subjected to the worst child abuse and neglect imaginable, and their drunken parents told me the children were a pain in the ass and hoped they died. It was only my partner's intervention, which kept me from punching the parents' tickets that hot summer afternoon.

So what's the point?

If you deal with the crap we do in this business over a long period of time without benefit of some form of outside support, you're headed for a major train wreck. For many of us the support keeping us sane comes from family and close friends (often of the non cop variety) if we're mature and smart enough to appropriately share our feelings and concerns with them. For others the needed support does, in fact, come from a faith in a supreme being, regardless of particular religion. Still others get the desired support from a combination of the two.

I'm not advocating every LEO "get religion" — it's a personal choice. For personal psychological and emotional survival every officer needs to find someone or some entity to rely on for support other than him/herself. Way back in 1624, the British poet John Donne wrote No Man Is An Island. His point was the one I wish to make. As human beings, even as tough cops, we should not, indeed cannot, bear all of life's burdens unassisted. Even, or perhaps especially, cops need and deserve the support of others when the going gets rough. Sure many of us would like to think we're the "one Ranger" that can handle "one riot" unassisted … but the reality is, we can't.

Far too many of us, particularly early in our careers, eat, breathe and live being a cop. There certainly is something addictive about the adrenaline rush that results from handling hot calls. I was as guilty as anyone of not letting go of the job during my off hours. Like others, I paid a price for that. We need healthy non-work related endeavors during our off-duty time; they contribute to the health, strength and sanity that serve us well during the hours we are at work. Part of the stay healthy equation is relaxation, a hobby or physical activity, and time spent with others whose ear we can bend if we need to.

Count yourself fortunate if you have a support system as suggested herein. If you don't, I suggest you develop one. And if you do, don't forget to say thanks from time to time — be it to your spouse, a close friend, or in the case of some of us a supreme being.

Be Safe Out There

There's not a chief or sheriff I know whom ever wants to experience the death of a department member ... ever. That's especially true if the loss is line of duty related. We all know a line of duty death (LODD) can happen anywhere, any time. Much of the content of American COP is devoted to articles designed to help every cop, every shift, every day come home safe and sound.

The holidays present some unique challenges to law enforcement officers in a number of ways, not the least of which has to do with survival. If you look at the statistics compiled over the years by the National Law Enforcement Memorial Foundation you might note January and December of each year are not without their losses of LEOs in the line of duty. I suspect the uniqueness of the holiday season may contribute to the LODDs we experience each year. Why do you suppose this is, and what might we do to minimize the tragedies occurring within our profession during this time of year?

Disturbing Trends

One of the trends I noticed when working the streets was the holidays seem to bring out either the best or worst in people. I've witnessed some extraordinary kindness and charity from ordinary people, but I've also seen the worst in people as the holiday season approaches. I'll never forget a murder-suicide I handled one year. A single father couldn't afford presents for his two children, so he put a single round from a .45 into each of their heads, penned a suicide note explaining his actions, and then took his own life.

In these very difficult economic times more people will be hard pressed to celebrate the holidays in ways they might prefer. We often hope incidents like this won't happen, but experience tells us they will. It's the officer on the street who has to deal with such events. And it's the officer on the street who must deal with the suicide by cop incidents, which are increasing in a time when many people cannot pay their bills, afford housing, and certainly cannot afford gifts for those who might expect them.

In some cases it's a legitimate despondency, which may cause them to harm others — including the law enforcement personnel called to handle incidents involving such people. It behooves each of us wearing a badge and carrying a firearm to be particularly cautious during a time of year and in a year where economic circumstances alone may result in an increase in such cases. And those same economic circumstances may mean fewer backup officers, as far too many police agencies have had to reduce their numbers.

You're Only Human

There's another side to this subject, which merits discussion. This season also impacts officers, not because of the actions of others, but due to personal circumstances within their own lives. Many of us have families with children and we too may be somewhat upset pay cuts and reduced overtime opportunities have forced us to cut back on gift giving.

The holiday season generally brings with it more social obligations; trips to visit extended family, hosting or attending holiday parties, finding time to go Christmas shopping, attempting to get time off or arrange a shift swap so not all of the holiday season will be spent working. These events in officers' lives can easily lead to frustration and distraction. And a distracted cop is a vulnerable cop. At a time when we're likely to encounter more than our fair share of despondent and potentially dangerous subjects on the street, we can ill afford to not be at the top of our game — mentally and tactically.

What's The Solution?

Given that we cannot control the mindset and motivations of others we may encounter on the street, it's to our advantage to position ourselves in the best place possible. We can do this by having frank discussions with family and loved ones about the limitations of the current economy on our ability to be generous. I bet they'll understand, and in doing so it relieves a lot of pressure and distraction, which would otherwise be on our shoulders.

Having a frank discussion can also soothe the pain of our absence from parties and family gatherings should time off or shift exchanges not be possible. And remember, relying on others for support isn't a bad idea either. It may help to remember "the reason for the season." So, while we can't control what the bad guys do; we can minimize self-distraction through frank discussions with family and friends. I encourage you to do so and wish you the best this holiday season.

Duty or Dishonor

I'm sure like many readers of American COP, I recently awoke to disturbing news carried by all of the mainstream media: An independent investigation into the 2009 Fort Hood massacre revealed that the FBI seriously dropped the ball. Specifically, the Bureau ignored Army Major Nidal Hasan's connections with known and suspected Islamic terrorists. Hasan brutally murdered 13 US soldiers and wounded 23 others in November 2009. The question in the minds of many was how such a person could have continued to serve as a military officer when he was known to have exchanged e-mails with extremists like Anwar al-Awlaki.

I no sooner finished reading the various media accounts, which summarized the verdict of the independent investigation, when I received e-mails from readers of this column asking me to devote column space to what one of them described as, "the greatest abandonment of law enforcement responsibility" in his lifetime. The independent investigation concluded political correctness deterred what would and should have been normal FBI practices and procedures when dealing with a "fellow traveler" such as Hasan. In short, the Bureau was so afraid of being criticized for focusing on a Muslim they failed to alert military authorities to the fact an Army officer could very well have been a threat to his fellow soldiers.

Fundamental Failures

Those who read this column on a regular basis know I vehemently object to political correctness within contemporary law enforcement. I don't know if the FBI requires its agents to read the Law Enforcement Code of Ethics before they graduate from Quantico or not. If not, they should. And if they do, they should take it seriously. As law enforcement officers, our fundamental duty is to protect mankind and we simply cannot do that by putting our heads in the sand, nor can we do it by being cowardly in our approach to the job.

Political correctness in our profession always has negative consequences. Generally, those consequences are poor morale within the agency and less than appropriate service to the public. In this case, political correctness indirectly, but very clearly, cost 13 innocent human beings their lives. By its failure to act on actionable intelligence for fear of being criticized, the Bureau failed in its duty to the American public. There's simply no other way to put it. Historically, law enforcement has been above politics and playing favorites depending on who holds a particular political office at a particular point in time. It's clear in this tragic case politics won over duty, and the results were both dishonor and death.

US Haters Club

Since history cannot be changed and there's no do-over that can restore life to the Fort Hood victims, I'd hope the FBI has learned a lesson; political correctness will yield to the basic responsibility the Bureau has long had and, in the past, met in a generally acceptable fashion. However, given the political climate of today I'm not at all sure much will change. Even more, since the political agenda of our current leadership impacts all federal law enforcement agencies, I'm concerned about something with far greater and more serious consequences than Fort Hood — the political correctness of the Department of Homeland Security when it comes to the issue of "OTM" (other than Mexican) illegal immigrants coming into the country.

In her meant for public deception role, DHS Secretary Napolitano denies the Border Patrol is encountering many illegals from countries which harbor terrorism, and from countries which have publicly declared their desire to inflict harm on the US. Yet, information from reliable sources within the Border Patrol, as well as that gathered by the media, especially along the US-Mexico border, it's quite clear Napolitano's words are anything but true.

Knowledge: A Two-Way Street

Fortunately over the past several decades, great advances have been made in our profession — in tactics and technology. Today's street cop has the potential to do more things quicker and more efficiently than any of us from prior generations in public service. Tactics have gone way beyond the old John Wayne approach to dealing with potentially violent confrontations. As much as I'm a fan of John Wayne, today's tactics are clearly much safer for all involved than the "single officer is expected to handle everything" approach of years past.

Modern technology is state-of-the-art. The ability to determine within seconds, due to automation, whether the subject of a field interview is a wanted and dangerous felon sure beats the 45 minutes I used to wait for a Wants and Warrants return in the early years of my career. The capability of rapidly breeching a door with explosives on a no-knock warrant for a dangerous suspect is something that, had it been in place a long time ago, would've saved the lives of many officers. I could go on, but undoubtedly readers who use state of the art tactics and technology are very aware of what's available to them. The question is: Are those above you in rank up to speed on what's in use? Why is it important they be current on practices in use? And, if they're not aware of what their officers are doing or using … whose responsibility is it to make sure they are?

Observing Others

As an agency head, I've always made a practice of watching how other chiefs and sheriffs respond during media briefings — particularly when they concern major incidents and, especially, officer involved shootings. My purpose has been to benefit from their experiences, to see the things they do right and the mistakes they make when dealing with the media. This, at best, can only be described as anti-law enforcement. Certainly I've observed briefings, which have made me proud to be part of our profession. Unfortunately, there are many times when I'm embarrassed for the agency head (and the profession in general) when a chief obviously lacks familiarity with the tactics and technology used by his or her own officers.

Watching administrators who use antiquated arguments and cite tactics and technology no longer in use, in an effort to defend the department's actions, tells me several things. First and foremost, it tells me the boss hasn't kept current on what his agency is doing and why.

Important? Yes. A lack of familiarity with current practices on the chief's part can have legal repercussions for the agency. Can you say vicarious liability? It can expose the involved officers to legal jeopardy if there's a conflict between what the chief thinks is accepted practice, and what the troops have obviously been taught. And regardless of any legal ramifications, it makes the agency look bad and erodes public confidence.

Things Change

What's the source of the sort of disconnect I'm talking about? It's really quite simple. The chief can't attend every SWAT, K-9, non-lethal weapons, or pursuit class his officers do. As a practical matter, some chiefs have never attended any such courses, and if they did they were probably years ago. As noted, things change — more and more quickly today than ever before. What the chief may have learned if and when he went through SWAT school is hugely different from what is taught today. I certainly know this is true in my case. So, how do we work around this disconnect?

There are only two ways I know of to rectify this particular problem. The chief must be astute enough to pick the brains of those who attend current training when they return from said training. The chief will then not only know what his troops are learning, he can determine whether the training will be implemented department wide, or is even consistent with department policy.

Finally, those attending the training should take the initiative in seeking some of the boss's time to give him a briefing on training content. Knowledge is a 2-way street, with both the person responsible for sending officers to training as well as those trained being on the same page. Keeping knowledge current and correct is in everyone's best interests.

Time to Revisit Recruitment

Let me say from the outset, I'm well aware that the majority of today's law enforcement officers are quality people and highly professional. I know this because I work with many of them. However, I believe it's fair and accurate to state that a minority, unfortunately an increasing minority, of officers are unfit for police service and should never have been hired in the first place; only by administrators ignoring their deficiencies did they complete probation. The two pertinent questions are: Why is this the case? What can/should we do about it?

As sometimes happens, my views on this subject may not sit well with some people, but then I don't view my goal as a columnist as winning any popularity contests.

Why?

We seem to have an increasing number of cops who never should've been hired in the first place. Is it because there's a shortage of applicants? In a few places, this may be the case. In all honesty, however, the number of applicants generally far exceeds the vacancies. What seems to be occurring in far too many agencies is that selection criterion focuses on meeting some sort of "quota" rather than selecting the best possible candidates. Perhaps this occurs in some jurisdictions because the agency cut a deal with the devil (the feds) and agreed to a set of hiring benchmarks based upon gender or ethnicity. To do that downsizes the pool of acceptable candidates to a level where, to meet the benchmarks, some watering down of formerly reasonable and accepted standards may have to occur.

Here are some examples. Formerly, little if any drug usage in an applicant's past was acceptable to law enforcement agencies. Today, however, in too many places the only disqualifier is "recent (within the past year) use of hard drugs." I know of several agencies that do not disqualify applicants based upon prior use of hallucinogenic drugs even though it's a well-known fact that undesirable side effects can spontaneously occur years after a drug's last use. The price paid in some agencies for hiring "former" druggies is on-duty theft or sale of drugs, or smuggling narcotics to inmates.

What about employing those with prior juvenile felony convictions, which may have been sealed or expunged? I know of one agency which has employed multiple officers with backgrounds that include the felony crime of assault with a deadly weapon. And then there are the unnamed but very prominent big city and county agencies that have somehow justified the hiring of "reformed" street gang members only to find they've developed their own criminal gangs within the agencies that have employed them. Chiefs and sheriffs are shocked such things can happen. Really?

Call me old school if you wish, but I can read about the relapse rates of alcoholics, druggies and gang bangers as well as anyone else. Do I think some of these offenders are cured? Yes, but the risks of employing them in certain jobs such as teachers and cops is just too great. Should such folks be denied employment opportunities? In some professions, yes, and law enforcement is one of those professions. Unlike "A" grades handed out freely to so many in our schools today, being sworn in as a cop is not a right to be given to just anyone. It's something which, for the integrity of the profession and the well-being of the public we serve, needs to be earned. And doing drugs, being a street gang member, or engaging in felony crimes does not earn it.

A Wealth of Candidates

There was once a time when the majority of new hires in our business were former members of the US military. Were they all cut out to be good cops? No. But many were, and they came without the baggage too many of today's applicants carry with them. Plus, they had some life experience, an understanding of chain of command

and above all a devotion to duty. I don't have a bias in this regard, as the closest I ever came to being in the military was a few years of ROTC in college.

As we downsize our military and back down our effort in Afghanistan (not saying we should, but that seems to be the direction we're headed in at the time of this writing) we are presented with a tremendous opportunity to add men and women to our ranks with the virtues and experience I just noted. I realize there are bad apples in the military too, but the majority is anything but bad. And, given the composition of the modern military, with many minorities and women distinguishing themselves by their service, it just might be possible to use the military as a recruitment base to meet the quota system so popular in some agencies. I certainly think it's worth the effort to bring them into our profession.

Slip-Slidin' Away

My law enforcement career, reserve and full time combined, is now rapidly approaching 50 years in length. That's a long time, and it certainly means I'm getting old, but all this experience doesn't necessarily mean I'm always right. It provides me with a basis for comparing how things used to be to how they are today — something newer members of our profession may not be able to do as readily. For example, I can compare the ills once characterizing law enforcement to the level of professionalism we've attained and, now, to a whole new set of ills that appear to be upon us.

Early in my career I worked in a high-crime rate minority population area of Los Angeles County. I had the opportunity to work with a deputy sheriff who was the very first of that particular minority to be assigned to my patrol station. From his accounts, as well as having grown up in the same area myself, I knew of the discrimination that used to occur. For much of the last century, law enforcement treated minority citizens differently than the majority population. Today, even the youngest members of our profession should have a feel for the ills that beset "pre-professional" law enforcement, as they're well documented in our history books.

From the early 1960s until the present day, law enforcement has made a concerted effort, largely successful, to become more professional. As a consequence, citizens should expect a fair and impartial exercise of authority with neither prejudice towards, nor preferential treatment of, people based upon race, ethnicity, national origin, religion or any other individual characteristic. Unfortunately, things seem to be in the process of changing and I find it reprehensible, doing a huge disservice to our nation and law enforcement.

What is this change? It's perhaps best described as reverse discrimination in which some people, based upon race, ethnicity or national origin are actually receiving preferential treatment, and it's all because of a fear on the part of some police leaders that we might offend someone. And given today's emphasis on political correctness (a term I'm tired of having to use), we certainly can't have that! Let me provide a few examples.

Oh My!

At the federal level is the much-discussed incident during a recent election when members of the New Black Panthers physically intimidated voters outside an election precinct. In the pre-professional era it might well have been KKK members intimidating blacks without any intervention by law enforcement. During what I call the era of professional law enforcement, cops would have intervened in any case of intimidation, but it's not so today in some places.

During the professional era of law enforcement, agencies at different levels of government worked together cooperatively and without politics or prejudices entering into the decision-making process. Sadly, this no longer appears to be the case. For example, LAPD Chief Charlie Beck recently announced his agency would not turn over illegal immigrants arrested for low-level crimes to ICE for deportation. He's also previously spoken in favor of issuing driver's licenses to illegals, too.

Recently, in a large Midwest city, Islamic protestors pelted a group of non-violent Christians with rocks and bottles, causing injuries to several. This behavior, amounting to a felony crime, was clearly and objectively captured on video by local media. Police were present yet did nothing to stop the assaults or apprehend those committing them. When asked why, the police spokesman stated they didn't want to further agitate the Islamists. So let me get this straight: People are assaulted, we do nothing and the net result is the criminals, not the victims, get preferential treatment. Really?

Danger! Warning!

These few examples (and there are many more), illustrate the slippery slope upon which our officers are being made to walk. When law enforcement leaders make enforcement decisions based upon who might be the subject of enforcement rather than on the basis of whether laws are being violated, we engage (in reverse) in the same sort of shameful and harmful discrimination, which occurred particularly in the South prior to the Civil Rights Act of 1964. Deciding whether to enforce laws on the books, or whether to assist another agency in doing so, based upon political considerations is patently unprofessional. If it keeps up and expands, as it appears to be doing, the professional reputation of all law enforcement, which took decades of hard work to build, will be destroyed much more quickly than it was created.

If chiefs or sheriffs have heartburn over the legitimacy of certain laws, they should seek to have those laws changed. To arbitrarily decide not to enforce laws with which they disagree (for any reason) is totally contrary to the oath of office we took when we entered this profession. In short order, the actions of law enforcement leaders who play politics rather than do police work will be the downfall of law enforcement, as many of us have known it. And it will erode the trust the majority of our citizens have placed in us.

A Case for Reserves

Like many readers I began my career as a reserve. In my case it was as a reserve deputy sheriff with a large agency in Southern California. As a chief I have always maintained a reasonably sized reserve program for the departments I have served. There are a number of reasons for that.

Let me say at the outset what I believe reserves are not. Reserves are not a substitute for regular, salaried officers. They should not be used to cover shifts that would otherwise be paid assignments for full-time personnel unless very extreme circumstances exist. They are, rather, a supplement to full-time staff. They are available to provide extra patrols when warranted, to "double up" single-officer patrol units for officer safety purposes, to assist with special events and to provide a pool of trained personnel during major incidents or anytime the proverbial bad stuff hits the fan.

We live and work in extremely difficult economic times. Many departments have had to reduce full-time staffing to ridiculously low and often unsafe levels. Some, as reported in past issues of American COP, have been forced due to budget catastrophes to staff almost their entire patrol force with reserves under the direction of only one or two salaried employees. I guess that shows the priorities of our elected officials, eh? Even in so-called normal economic times there are lots of pluses for a cadre of dedicated, well-trained reserves.

The Two Reserves

Drawing on my own experience, there are two types of people who become reserves — and both are valuable resources. The first type is the person who has full-time employment elsewhere, perhaps in a professional field, and who doesn't desire to become a full-time cop. This person can be motivated by the excitement and variety, which from time to time characterizes what we do. Or, this person may be motivated by the desire to serve his or her community. Career

Reserves, as they're often called, can bring stability, maturity and experience to a reserve program.

The second type of reserve is often seeking a full-time law enforcement position and views their service as a reserve as getting a foot in the door. Whatever the motivation, every reserve potentially expands public support for law enforcement. Reserves, like we regulars, have friends and family who, if they weren't already, become "pro law enforcement" by virtue of the reserve's endeavors. And that is a good thing.

I've always sought to balance my reserve program with both types of people. Through their stability, career reserves can serve as a positive example to the less experienced. Those desiring to become regular full-time officers offer an excellent recruitment base when filling full-time vacancies. In fact, with the last two departments I headed I never hired a full-time officer who wasn't one of our reserves. Let's look at the advantages of that.

First, if someone isn't cutting it as a reserve he won't remain in the reserve program. Reserves are "at will" volunteers and those who fail to meet standards are simply not retained. We get to know our reserves and their strengths, weaknesses and potential. On the flip side, reserves get to know the department as well and if they sense the fit isn't good, they won't stay. So, we wind up with a group the department is confident in, and reserves who are confident in the department. If a vacancy occurs, a reserve who applies knows exactly what sort of agency he is seeking employment with and the department knows very clearly what sort of applicant the reserve is.

Benefit-Rich

The benefits of hiring from the reserve corps are numerous. In fact, I have yet to see a downside to such a practice. Turnover due to dissatisfaction on the part of the agency or the newly hired officer is practically nonexistent. Once academy training is completed, the

FTO program is usually much smoother as the new hire is already familiar with many department policies and procedures and has already been accepted by the people with whom he will work.

In short, there are far fewer surprises with reserves-turned-regulars than with an unknown hire as officer. From all perspectives, economic and otherwise, an investment in developing and maintaining a highly competent reserve corps is clearly in the agency's best interests. Try it ... you will likely see the value.

An Intentional, Subtle, and Damaging Change?

The Law Enforcement Officers Code of Ethics has existed for decades. I'm old as dirt and when I became a Los Angeles County Deputy Sheriff in the 60s we took the oath early on in the academy. It was impressed upon us just how important adherence to the oath would be throughout our careers. While there is some question as to where the oath originated, it's generally attributed to the Superintendent of the New York State Police who compiled it from multiple sources in 1930.

Although the origin is debatable the intent and content are not. It's unfortunate the International Association of Chiefs of Police (IACP) has chosen to modify the long-standing code of ethics and call it, instead, an oath of honor. IACP's position is not surprising. Based upon its track record, the organization is very much like the United Nations. It's principally supported by US dollars and does little more than provide cover for the personal agendas of too many of its members.

Honored Excuses

The differences between ethics and honor are substantial, and the IACP focus on the latter rather than the former goes a long way toward explaining what is increasingly wrong with police leadership today. The code of ethics is based upon a set of moral values and prescribes a set of rules of behavior as well as expectations for those who subscribe to the oath. The law enforcement code of ethics, as originally written and followed for decades, was based upon the exact same moral principles that serve as the foundation for our Constitution and Bill of Rights.

A code of honor is substantially different, indeed much more watered down from the original. By definition, honor means those taking the code admire and revere the content but (and this is critical) do not swear to abide by the content. Ethics has with it an obligation. Honor allows for excuses. Let's look for a moment at how these not so subtle differences play out in the real world of law enforcement.

The oath mandates respect for the US Constitution — all of it — not just those parts with which a particular practitioner happens to agree with. The Second Amendment to the Constitution is still valid law and, for those of us who subscribed to the oath, we are duty bound to support it. Those who simply honor certain values are under no obligation to support the Constitution. Thus we find an increasing number of so-called police leaders who are openly antigun and who do all they can to restrict the rights of citizens in that regard. Doubt me? Try and get a concealed carry permit in any of the liberal bastions of our nation. It's generally the top cops who subscribe to the oath of honor and not the oath of ethics who lead these locales.

The oath says we will keep our private lives unsullied. Those who simply honor certain principles are under no obligation to lead an exemplary life, and it shows. Witness the police leaders who in decades past would have been terminated for improprieties such as DUI, sexual harassment or spousal abuse, but who today keep their jobs and think nothing of their violation of the public trust.

The oath says we will never let personal feelings influence our decisions. Yet in multiple jurisdictions today agency leaders, based upon their personal feelings, have declined to enforce laws such as those requiring all drivers have valid licenses and certain vehicles must be impounded. Perhaps they think, "But that's okay, since I never took an oath requiring me to enforce the law. I just said I'd honor certain principles as long as I found doing so to be in my personal best interests."

The oath says "with no compromise for crime and with relentless prosecution of criminals I will enforce the law ..." Oath takers cannot justify ignoring the numerous and often felonious crimes committed by "occupiers." Those who simply honor certain principles find it very easy to ignore violations of law in order to remain popular. I could cite an almost limitless number of examples in which police leaders operate as if the Code of Ethics never existed. But they'll quickly justify their actions by citing the fact they honor certain principles. To them, honor is not synonymous with obey.

The erosion of values within police leadership didn't suddenly develop overnight. It took decades. If we're ever able (and I pray we will be) to restore the adherence to the Code of Ethics so critical to true professionalism, it will likely take a few more decades to accomplish. Unless each and every one of us commits ourselves to adhering to the time honored Code of Ethics many of us subscribed to at the outset of our careers, it will never happen. And, both law enforcement and society as a whole will continue to suffer because of it.

Loss of Public Favor?

A reader recently forwarded me a brief article from an online law enforcement-related blog dealing with the question of whether law enforcement is losing the public's favor. The reader asked me to comment on it, so hence this column.

Law enforcement today is caught between a rock and a hard place when it comes to the issue of public trust, respect and favor. It's a dilemma not easily solved because law enforcement policies, procedures, focus and actions, while pleasing to some, will be upsetting to others. To really examine the issue we must look at two things.

What is, or at least should be, the real purpose of police work? What do the majority of people in today's society want of their police? It's fair to say the answers to these two questions are quite different. Therefore, depending on whether an agency chooses to focus on the real purpose of our business or accommodating the wishes of the majority, public perception will be effected either positively or adversely.

Our Purpose

From my perspective, and at times I think I'm in the minority, the purpose of our profession is to protect people from those who would prey on them through criminal behavior. Sure, we provide non-enforcement services as well, but the bottom line is other entities can do that. Only law enforcement is entrusted with the power of arrest and the authority to use deadly force for the protection of innocents. The question is whether or not the majority of the public really wants this to be our role. A look at how our electoral process played out recently will help answer the question.

What did last November's election tell us? Lots of things, not the least of which is that we live in an increasingly "it's all about me, what have you done for me lately?" society. It's a society in which the majority of citizens, as expressed by their vote, want fewer things to be illegal (witness the votes in multiple states just on the issue of legalized marijuana alone) and more free stuff to be given to them. It's a society that prefers its law enforcers to turn a blind eye to issues such as illegal immigration, driving while unlicensed or operating uninsured and unregistered vehicles. It's a society that has opted for a watering down of the Constitutional framework that in the past provided the boilerplate under which cops operate.

Popular Vote?

So where does all of this leave us? Well for those agencies viewing their primary purpose as arresting bad guys and taking a hard line against activities the law still classifies as criminal, they'll please the minority of our citizens — at least as that minority position was expressed at the ballot box. However, they will not please the majority who view strict enforcement of the law as an infringement on their freedom. Those who lead agencies following the time-honored precepts of our profession will likely not survive in this political climate — those who are "more understanding, compassionate, reasonable and flexible" will replace them. And they will be replaced by the spineless, politically correct who share the same liberal perspective as their constituents.

As we've already seen over the past decade, other agencies will adopt a much less enforcement-oriented philosophy and practice. They will enjoy a high degree of "public trust" because of their soft and, at times, hands-off approach to dealing with criminal behavior. It will take some time before people recognize, if ever, there is a strong correlation between soft policing and increases in crime. But then, given how the majority voted in the last presidential election, I suspect the majority are either too naïve or have consumed too much Kool-Aid to care.

The result of this dichotomy is we'll likely be left with aggressive, traditional policing agencies perhaps not well trusted by many, but who will maintain low crime rates and safe communities in which to live and work. On the flip side, and unfortunately this already applies to too many large cities in the US, will be cities and counties where cops are well liked, but with violent crime rates bursting through the roof. Not the sort of place I'd want to live, and certainly not the type of department I could ever lead. But people get what they ask for — and deserve — I think the next 4 years in particular will prove that.

Who Speaks for Us?

I must be more of an old-school Neanderthal than most people say, because the voices which once spoke for police leaders in this country no longer speak for me. It concerns me when organizations of so-called police chief executives ramble in such a manner it sounds like they're choking on a mouthful of left-wing Kool-Aid. It's bad enough when individual police leaders grab headlines through statements that make it clear they've forgotten their oath of office. When organizations such as the IACP and the California Police Chiefs Association go off the deep end, I fear for the future of our profession.

The major issue causing me heartburn with these two organizations, and others like them, is their position on how to control gun violence; it's not the only issue however. When dealing with gun-related issues, these organizations have adopted, without reservation or modification, President Obama's position — certain types of weapons and magazines of certain capacity will, if made illegal, bring an end to such things as school shootings.

Any street cop worth his salt knows that is patently false.

The truth is it's not the tool, but the fool who uses it, at the root of the problem. A nut job intent on harming someone will use whatever weapon or device is available. Similarly, nut jobs or hard-core criminals will not eliminate "assault weapons" (whatever those are) or hi-cap magazines from their arsenals. In fact, only the law abiding who wouldn't commit a random mass murder in the first place will be penalized. You would think organizations at least theoretically composed of honest, objective, ethical, experienced "leaders" would tell it like it is, not like they think others would prefer they tell it. That appears to not be the case.

Hands-Off

In addition to "gun control" — which frankly, I view as being more about "law-abiding citizen control" — there are other issues major law enforcement associations have taken positions about that would have been unheard of just a decade ago.

In case no one has noticed, unlawful entry into the United States across our international borders is still a crime. Yet not only do many individual police chiefs (very few sheriffs, thank goodness) adamantly refuse to enforce the laws against illegal entry appropriately, they have adopted a hands-off posture on just about any enforcement related to illegal aliens. They certainly wouldn't want to be accused of being insensitive or, much worse, engaging in racial profiling.

Some police chiefs have gone so far as to provide special treatment toward the "undocumented," refusing to enforce state motor vehicle registration and insurance laws (Los Angeles) if the offenders happen to be illegal aliens. They, of course, have no reluctance to enforce those same laws against US citizens. Where I come from that's known as discrimination, and was once something police leaders and the associations representing them would have done anything to avoid. No longer the case.

Organizational Advantages

So — and I'm not alone in this regard — what is a police leader to do if the associations and organizations which once responsibly represented them no longer do so? Remain the "Lone Ranger" without any organizational memberships? Some will choose that path though, and I've found over the years belonging to the proper sort of organization or association has several advantages. One distinct advantage is the fact there's strength in numbers, and that can be extremely important when there's a need. One need might be to push legislation truly needed by the profession and the public we serve.

Second, collegial relationships among police leaders are a good thing. Others with more experience or expertise in a particular area can be networked with via mutual organizational membership. I know in my career as a chief I've use the knowledge possessed by others on more than one occasion, to the benefit of my department and the people I serve.

I try to stay abreast of what options are out there in terms of representing what I view as the mainstream of policing philosophy. Frankly, the associations once fitting the bill in that regard no longer do so. There are only two organizations related to leadership within the profession that, philosophically, I can advocate. One is composed not only of law enforcement, but military members as well as others, and is focused on adherence to the oaths of office we took (which some of us actually remember and try to adhere to). The other is primarily, but not exclusively, an association of sheriffs. There are, however, a number of us non-sheriff types who proudly belong.

Alternative Thoughts

I must clearly note my recommendations represent my opinion and do not state or imply the endorsement of American COP Magazine or its publisher. Oathkeepers (www.oathkeepers.org) and the Constitutional Sheriffs and Peace Officers Association (www.cspoa.org) are the only two professional organizations focusing on organizational leadership I've found which adhere to the ethics, duties and responsibilities upon which our profession has historically been based. I commend them to your attention, and at the same time invite readers who may know of other reputable police leadership-related associations to please let me know of their existence.

Make It Realistic

The state in which I reside establishes standards for both regular and reserve law enforcement officers and provides one training academy that all full-time peace officers in the state must attend. In terms of training law enforcement personnel other than full-time sworn officers, the specifics are left to the individual agencies. This has, in the case of reserves, community service officers and other "civilian" classifications, resulted in a lack of standardization. It also prevents personnel from adjoining agencies from working effectively with their peers in other jurisdictions (even those with the same job classification) in mutual aid incidents.

Several years ago, the police chiefs and sheriffs in five contiguous counties in the eastern portion of the state collaborated to correct this training and standardization deficiency. Through much negotiation with the state standards and training department, they obtained approval to develop and provide a regional training academy, which initially focused on standardized training for reserve police officers and sheriff's deputies. This approach has been expanded to include the training of SWAT medics (fire department paramedics assigned to the regional SWAT team) as well as some non-sworn positions such as Community Service Officers.

Keeping It Real(istic)

Because of the perception that I had some time on my hands, I was asked to consider coordinating this regional training effort following its first offering in 2012. I consented, in great measure because I've rarely found anything in this profession more satisfying than helping to mold and train those who are our future. In looking over the curriculum used in the first regional academy session, I found it to be both comprehensive and relevant to the duties the graduates would most likely be assigned upon return to their agencies. With input from others I found, however, some of the more important subjects were a bit too theoretical, too CYA (cover-your-ass) oriented and not realistic in what the graduates were likely to encounter on the street.

As a result of our curriculum analysis, we shortened some courses, lengthened others and added some courses, extending the academy by one week. The focus was placed on making the training as realistic and relevant as possible for the reserves and paraprofessionals who would be attending. Feedback has been extremely positive, which we expected it would be, as our training model follows very much the same lines as presented by the various experts who write for this magazine.

Defensive tactics is a critical skill for anyone in our profession. Too often it's taught not as much from the perspective of keeping our officers safe and injury free, as it is from the perspective of not getting the agency sued. Our course doesn't teach, advocate or condone excessive force, and it doesn't focus on a mechanical application of, for example, takedowns following an "A-B-C" step-by-step approach. It focuses on getting the task accomplished as quickly and as humanely as possible. In short, it's realistic. The same can be said for our approach to firearms training. All the theory in the world is just fine if your goal is to write an instruction manual. If the desired end result is neutralizing a threat, which legally, ethically and morally must be neutralized, realism rather than theory is the order of the day.

Effective Supportive Roles

We included courses to make the part-time professional and paraprofessional personnel more effective in incidents in which their participation is not that of a star player, but is nevertheless critical to the success of the mission. In pursuit of that goal we included the course "Introduction to SWAT", in which the commander of the regional SWAT team served as instructor. Everyone knows the reserve or paraprofessional's role in a SWAT incident is most likely going to be somewhere on the outer perimeter. Yet, we also know if said employee fails to do his or her job properly, the end result could be both disastrous and dangerous for those in more critical positions.

Hearing from the SWAT Commander how vital each person's role is to the success of the overall mission made a positive difference in the students' self-image. It was also helpful for the students to understand what the likely sequence of events might be in a barricaded suspect incident. Knowing in advance, for example, the "pops and bangs" they might hear could be either gunfire or the activation of pyrotechnic distraction devices gave them a realistic view of what to expect.

Those entering our profession today, even through part-time or paraprofessional channels, are smart and discerning people. They often have a pretty good handle on the "textbook" before they ever enter the classroom at our training facilities. What they need and deserve from us as their mentors is a healthy dose of realism.

It May Be Legal, But...

I'm not an attorney nor am I a legal scholar. I'm also not one who opposes the reasonable, necessary and prudent use of technology to solve crimes. I've always found great satisfaction in putting bad guys in bracelets and taking them to jail. However my sixth sense, which has served me well since the '60s when I was pushing a black and white around south-central Los Angeles, is causing a very queasy feeling in the pit of my stomach. I sense a pending condition red for the future of what this nation has always stood for. And the biggest knot in my gut is because I perceive the profession I love being subtly lured into violating the rights of average, law-abiding US citizens. Let me explain.

Everyone's Under Suspicion

Much has been said and written over the past few months about the data mining being conducted by the National Security Administration (NSA). It's occurred under the cover of preventing terrorist acts, thus earning the judicial seal of approval making it legal. The domestic use of drones — some operated by law enforcement — is technology intended to "prevent crime and, when crimes occur, lead to swift apprehensions of those responsible." A number of cities, using DHS grants, are installing surveillance cameras throughout their jurisdictions. Why? To deter criminals and, again, to help solve crimes caught on video.

License Plate Reader (LPR) technology is a boon to those agencies that can afford it. Certainly the ability to automatically scan, read, query and determine if a particular vehicle is stolen or been used in a serious crime is viewed by the technology's proponents as beneficial. LPR technology allows for vehicles with expired registration to be flagged, yet many jurisdictions opt out of this particular use or mandate that expired registration "hits" not be acted upon. Why? Because of political correctness in many places where a high percentage of those enjoying defacto amnesty operate their vehicles with expired registration.

More recently, again thanks to DHS money, a number of police agencies are establishing checkpoints and motorists stopped are asked if they'll voluntarily give a DNA sample to be maintained in a database for investigatory use. I know what my response to such a question would be. Not only no, but hell no! It would be my answer even though I have no intention of ever committing a criminal act.

Then there's the TSA. Frankly, I see them as little more than an expensive make-work project allowing too many people to exert too much authority over the elderly, infirm, disabled, infants and small children. Like too many other things in our feel-good society today, it's mostly show and very little go.

All of the aforementioned uses of technology have been determined to be legal either under the Patriot Act or because public places are involved wherein there's no reasonable expectation of privacy. Individually, perhaps none of these things are offensive or inconsistent with the principles upon which this nation was founded. Collectively, they create an atmosphere and an attitude, which is anything but supportive of the Constitution and Bill of Rights.

Losing Our Way

I don't know about you, but I know exactly why I became a professional peace officer in the first place. It was to protect and serve. To put real bad guys — against whom I'd developed probable cause — in jail. I did not become a cop to contribute to a climate in which the average, law-abiding citizen was treated with suspicion, placed under surreptitious surveillance and made to feel guilty until proven innocent. I especially didn't become a cop to contribute to that perception/reality based upon a person's political or religious beliefs.

What disturbs me the most is the fact that far too many police agencies have begun to emulate what they see DOJ, FBI, IRS and NSA agents doing. And given the recent track record of those federal agencies, I don't consider this a good thing at all. While they may be acting in a legal fashion, the tone of many recent federal investigations and activities has been in conflict with the intent of our Founding Fathers. For local law enforcement to copy the federal example is to do the law-abiding citizens — whom we serve — a disservice.

My concern is for the potential to abuse and misuse all of the bits, bytes and other data modern technology can collect on our behalf. Clearly the IRS, for example, misused technology for political purposes. Who's to say local law enforcement won't be tempted to commit the same sin? With so many so-called police leaders putting political correctness and personal power ahead of oath of office it's bound to happen. The day it does, the destruction of our constitutional republic is almost guaranteed … and law enforcement will have aided and abetted it. Not my idea of protecting and serving.

Can Something Be Too Good?

I generally leave matters of weapons craft to the experts — folks like Clint Smith and others — who share their wisdom and knowledge with readers. However, for some time now, one aspect of officer survival has been bugging me, and as a chief I have the ethical obligation to share my concern with the troops as it may be directly related to their walking away healthy at the end of an armed confrontation.

Two events have prompted me to put these thoughts in writing. One was an account I recently read concerning an officer seriously wounded by gunfire who, as a result of being struck in his gun hand, was unable to draw his service weapon with his off hand and return fire. The second was a very informal study I conducted with a handful of officers at a recent handgun qualification session.

Solve One Problem ...

Back in the old days, the choices officers had regarding service weapons and the holsters to carry them were limited at best. This is no longer the case. While the semi-automatic pistol replaced the revolver as the primary weapon of choice long ago, the number of makes, models and calibers available to officers today is mind-boggling. Along with the weapon comes the choice of holsters, with the weapon retention level of those holsters ranging from minimum to extraordinary.

The holster's capability for retaining the weapon, unless the officer carrying it follows an exact procedure, has the benefit of minimizing the weapon being removed by a suspect intent on injuring or killing the officer. That's an obvious plus. The downside is that given a particular holster's design, its placement on the gun belt and the amount of other equipment carried on the belt it may prove impossible for an officer whose strong hand/arm is injured to quickly, if at all, draw the weapon with the off hand. Such a delay or inability to draw with the "weak" hand could, as in the case I read about, cost the officer his or her life.

The increasingly popular use of exterior vest carriers by uniformed officers may make drawing with the off hand even more difficult. In such equipment, the bullet-resistant vest is worn in a carrier over the uniform shirt rather than under it. The carrier is designed to hold a variety of essential items in addition to the ballistic resistant vest. Handcuffs, OC, radio, flashlight, pens, notebook, etc., are finding their way into such exterior vest carriers.

The upside of such equipment is that when an officer is in the station doing reports, the entire vest carrier can be removed, thus eliminating a great deal of weight and allowing the officer to write reports in comfort. The vest can be donned in a hurry if necessary. The other plus is, according to some studies, wearing of this piece of equipment saves wear, tear and strain on the hips and back.

But the downside can be fatal.

...Create a New Problem

With so much bulk in the way, the offhand can barely reach the strong-side holster. My informal survey at the range proved precisely that. When officers were asked if they could draw their weapon with their off hand, all replied in the affirmative. Yet, five out of six were unable to demonstrate a successful draw and the sixth took forever to accomplish the task. Each of the officers involved in this little exercise were carrying holsters with the maximum retention capability currently available. Scary stuff.

Three of those officers have since changed to retention holsters enabling an off- or weak-hand draw. The other three (I recommend this as a good tactic in any event) have begun carrying backup firearms, which are securely carried in their vest carriers, and can be readily drawn with either hand.

As much as I laud the many improvements in the law enforcement equipment arena, experience over a long period of time has shown the need for caution. In some cases, such as some (but not all) retention holsters, a piece of equipment can be extremely good at one thing, and not good at all in others. While I'm not on the street in uniform every day, when I am I choose a retention holster, which allows for off-hand draw in a reasonable timeframe. And yes, I always carry a backup gun. Be safe.

Too Much Stuff

A previous column ("Can Something Be Too Good?", December 2013) prompted a lot of e-mails, most of which were in agreement with my opinion. My concern was that the amount of equipment carried by officers, particularly if carried in external vest carriers, could make it difficult and time-consuming (if not altogether impossible) to draw the duty sidearm with the off-hand if their dominant hand was disabled.

Another chief asked an even more basic question: What affect (if any) would eliminating some of the less-lethal equipment currently carried by most officers have, and would it create liability issues? Does an officer really need a baton and a chemical agent and an ECD as less-lethal options to a sidearm or patrol rifle?

Onerous Options

I don't think there's any question the more items officers are required to carry; the more cumbersome it is to access any individual item — especially under stressful conditions. Reducing the amount of equipment will help solve the dilemma discussed previously and the weight officers must lug around. Even more importantly, fewer weapon choices may facilitate timely decision-making, and thus, potentially save the life of an officer or innocent person.

In today's policing environment I don't think it's reasonable not to have a less-lethal option available on an officer's gun belt for use when such deployment is appropriate. But some agencies seem to subscribe to the theory: "if one's good, more's better." I'm not so sure about that. In some use of force situations, a transition must be made from less lethal to deadly force if it's justified. If it isn't then naturally having multiple less-lethal options may prove advantageous. But there are times when none of the less lethal devices are effective on a given person. In such cases we can only hope there are enough officers present to simply overpower the suspect and get him in restraints.

The decision of how many of these devices to carry is best left to each department — better yet, the individual officers — with the requirement at least one device of their choice be carried. Officers may elect to carry multiple devices, but there are caveats. Proficiency must be demonstrated and maintained with each device and they must understand there isn't a requirement to try every less-lethal option before transitioning to deadly force if warranted. Carrying multiple less-lethal options should not result in a potentially deadly delay (either in decision making or physical access) in transitioning.

Here's A Thought

I know of a police agency that very sensibly addressed their concerns about their officers being required to carry too much stuff. The agency's legal advisor opined that downsizing from three required less-lethal devices to one would not adversely impact liability if the argument could be made that the chosen device was generally effective. It's been proven that no single less-lethal tool is always effective. The attorney also speculated that if given a choice of tools, not every officer would choose the same one. Thus, at an incident in which multiple officers are involved, there's a likelihood more than one less-lethal option would be present — not all three carried by each individual officer. It's something to consider.

Where I work we have severe winters with sub-freezing temperatures likely six months out of the year. Our agency allows officers to select which device(s) they wish to carry. Several officers opt for an ECD during the warmer months when people aren't wearing multiple layers of heavy clothing, which will likely render the ECD ineffective. During winter months, most carry OC spray and a collapsible baton. This approach makes sense to me.

A lot of what we do and much of the equipment we use in this business are reasonable compromises. There are no guarantees in life and that extends to the effectiveness of any particular type of less-lethal device. Every officer should carry one device with which he's proficient; this will prevent the decision-making process from being so cumbersome it becomes dangerous. What do you think?

Selling the Advantages

As a former SWAT member and team commander I've watched with great interest the growth in sophistication of SWAT tactics over the years. I've also observed with interest the necessary and appropriate use of technology designed to enhance the safety of all, including citizens, during high-risk incidents. As my recent columns will attest, I'm not unaware of the perception a growing number of citizens have that law enforcement is becoming too militarized.

They're concerned civilian law enforcement is becoming an adversary rather than those who protect and serve. The issue we face is one of balancing the legitimate need for the maximum level of protection possible while reassuring law-abiding citizens the tools we use are for their benefit.

Perhaps no aspect of SWAT has caused more concern for the public than our use of armored vehicles. While vehicles such as the Lenco BEAR and BearCat have been in place in many jurisdictions for years, the recent availability of surplus military vehicles, like the MRAP (Mine Resistant Ambush Protection), has proven to be another ball game entirely. Excess property programs have enabled many jurisdictions too small to qualify for urban initiative grants to obtain needed protective vehicles. Commercially manufactured SWAT vehicles are intimidating enough to naïve citizens; MRAPs takes the intimidation factor up a few notches considering the images of their use on the battlefields in Iraq and Afghanistan. Whose responsibility is it to sell the need for and desirability of such vehicles to the general public? And of equal importance, how do we do it?

Understanding Perceptions

An agency with which I am familiar recently acquired an MRAP in near perfect condition through the Excess Property Program. It had been painted flat black, outfitted with equipment needed to support a regional SWAT team and marked to reflect its law enforcement ownership. Prominent among the markings, and consistent with what many agencies have incorporated into their vehicle labeling, was the word "RESCUE."

This prompted a rather critical and cynical outburst from some in the community whose level of suspicion that their local law enforcement was part of a DHS-FEMA "plot" was exacerbated by the arrival of this vehicle. The negative impression some people had as a result of this vehicle's appearance became a widely discussed and politicized issue. It needed to be countered before public sentiment caused local politicians to deny the funding needed to keep this valuable asset in operation.

This MRAP was intended from the outset to serve multiple counties and several municipalities in a region of nearly 10,000 square miles. Convincing the public of the need for this asset and offsetting public fears and misconceptions would only be accomplished if the sheriffs and police chiefs whose agencies would benefit from the vehicle spoke to the issue in unison and with well-reasoned arguments. Those arguments needed to address concerns of the laymen — to simply rely on the tactical advantages such a vehicle provides to SWAT operators wouldn't be convincing.

The law enforcement leaders in the region took the responsibility of "selling the product" by speaking as one to their constituents within their local communities. Next, they had to figure out how to sell it, and that required some thought and research.

Do Your Homework

While many of us in law enforcement think of such vehicles as: Providing protection to our personnel going into a hot zone, facilitating entry into a fortified structure and insertion of robots and/or chemical agents into a structure, they're not selling points to use on a skeptical public and in particular, politicians. What does sell is showing its use is a direct benefit to citizens. In the case of the entity I'm using as an example, they discovered a rather surprising number of recent incidents across the country in which armored vehicles were used to rescue injured and downed citizens and, even more frequently, evacuate citizens from structures adjacent to a shooter's location when there was absolutely no other safe way to accomplish such evacuations. These proved to be excellent selling points, particularly since in the incidents occurring in major metropolitan areas, television news crews captured the use of armored vehicles to evacuate innocents on video. Watching the videos proved very convincing even to the greatest of skeptics.

Because of a perception on the part of at least some of the public that specialized law enforcement units such as SWAT are being trained for public suppression if martial law is declared, we need to be sensitive to their concerns. More importantly, we need to explain our tactics and equipment — particularly those perceived as intimidating — from the perspective of how it serves them rather than oppresses them.

Is "Tactical" Overworked?

Is there anyone besides me who thinks we may have reached the point where "tactical" as a description of what we wear, carry and how we work is perhaps becoming just a bit overused? Or, in some cases, misused? Make no mistake of where I'm coming from. In addition to believing in the survival mindset, I'm a strong advocate for those things we can legally use and do that give us a "tactical" advantage when dealing with serious bad guys. I'm a bit concerned that in addition to being used as a marketing tool (justifying higher prices), the word "tactical" is giving too many cops a false, and thus potentially dangerous, sense of security as they go about their business.

Making Appearances

I recently watched a relatively new officer as he prepared to begin his patrol shift. His weapon was adorned with aftermarket tactical grips and a tactical light — great if they give him a better grip and he can see better in dark places. He was also wearing a very expensive pair of tactical boots, which again, is not a problem if they provide him with a higher level of protection.

Sticking out noticeably from behind his magazine pouches was a tactical knife … not a folder, but a fixed blade. I looked at it from the perspective of a potential adversary and thought how easy it would be for even an old guy like me to relieve him of it. I've always carried a knife on-duty and off; it's easily accessible but its location is not advertised to a potential assailant.

Carefully enclosed in his external, tactical vest carrier was a 50′ piece of paracord and a couple of packs of blood clot material. I carry both too, but my paracord is on my wrist in the form of a survival strap. I've not had occasion to use either on-duty, but it's better to have them and not need them than not have them in a moment of need.

Perched at a rakish angle atop the front of his head was a pair of what appeared to be rather expensive sunglasses. I actually asked him about those and he proudly told me they were ballistic rated and quite expensive. Whatever floats your boat I guess …

What Tactics?

Not an hour after this officer went into service I happened to be behind him on a main street in town; he activated his overhead emergency lights and made a traffic stop. It wasn't until after he made contact with the driver and returned to his vehicle that he got on the radio and called in the stop. This department doesn't have GPS-linked MCT's allowing stops to be "called in" with the push of a button. I pulled in behind him and covered him until the stop was completed and he was back in service.

What I saw from this one young officer in the space of an hour got me thinking. The "tactics" he used (or didn't use) on the traffic stop were dangerous. Is it possible with all the tactical accessories he was carrying he succumbed to the deadly sin of thinking all that stuff made him invincible? And if this were the case, how many other officers across the country subconsciously think that with the right amount and type of tactical equipment, tactical thinking and tactical planning aren't as necessary as they once were?

Know the Difference

I made it a point to visit with the officer soon after the stop and asked him why he failed to call in the stop before he made it. His excuse was that the radio was busy. I reminded him the stop was for an equipment violation, thus there was no urgency in making the stop. He could've and should've delayed the stop for the few seconds it took for the air to clear. We discussed the tactics involved in safe traffic stops.

Perhaps tactics aren't as glamorous as the tactical pen, light, boots, knife, etc. he'd invested so much money in. But, in the big order of things, all the tactical "stuff" in the world will do no good if tactical mindset and tactical decision-making are overlooked. You can't buy good tactics and you should know the difference between "tactics" and "tactical."

I regularly teach at a regional law enforcement training academy. I appreciate the opportunity to meet and talk with those entering this profession, which a few years down the road I'll be leaving. I'm generally impressed by the enthusiasm, motivation and dedication of those just starting out, but I sense from many of them the same reversed priorities I observed in the officer on the traffic stop. Their focus of attention seems to be on "stuff": What weapon? What retention holster? What patrol light? Which boots? Which gloves? All good questions, but I really wish they, and all the more experienced fellow cops, would focus on tactical thinking — first.

Are We Misusing SWAT?

In his article "Rise of the Warrior Cop" (Wall Street Journal, July 22, 2013) Radley Balko offers the opinion that, for a variety of reasons, some law enforcement agencies have become too militarized and are using SWAT resources in incidents not justified in their usage. Several American COP readers, who I happen to know to be excellent SWAT Commanders with their current agencies, asked if I'd read the article and comment on it here.

One of the highlights of my career was the time I spent as a SWAT team leader and later as a team commander. My initial SWAT training came from those who pioneered the concept on the Los Angeles County Sheriff's Department simultaneous with LAPD's invention of SWAT in the late 1960's. To this day I follow developments and issues related to SWAT with great interest.

I'm not a particular fan of Mr. Balko and don't agree with his underlying "agenda" in the topics he writes about. In this case, however, I think he offered several valid points, which those currently responsible for SWAT teams ought to consider. His first point, and he illustrates it with examples, is using SWAT "for effect" to conduct raids on such things as backroom gambling operations. Secondly is the use of SWAT in situations where that resource is not really needed for the sole purpose of justifying the expense of the resource.

Evolution

In the initial years following SWAT's creation, its intended and most frequent use was in barricaded suspect incidents, particularly those in which hostages were taken. I doubt anyone would argue against the use of SWAT in such situations and if they did they should be ignored. Today we often use a different approach to active shooters other than a full complement of SWAT personnel — it's the nature of the growth and evolution of tactical responses.

Over time SWAT has come to be utilized in pre-planned events such as high-risk warrant services, takedowns of marijuana grows and other incidents in which the probability of armed suspects/resistance is high. This is certainly justifiable, prudent and an efficient and effective use of a highly trained, specially equipped resource.

What cannot be justified — and where I agree with Balko — is using SWAT in low-risk incidents simply to justify the existence of the team and the costs of maintaining it. Using them to break up a gambling game simply because gambling happens to be a crime, particularly when undercover operatives involved in the game have identified no weapons threat, is a misuse of the resource.

You don't use a bulldozer when a hammer will do.

Costly Elitism

There are several downsides to using SWAT in situations where the risk of armed resistance (which is certainly always a possibility) is minimal. Primarily it's not cost effective. Mobilizing an entire team with all of its logistics and support equipment is expensive. Secondly, and perhaps of greater importance, it sends a very negative message to the rest of the department. The unnecessary use of SWAT tells patrol officers and detectives they're not viewed as competent to handle such situations.

Using the team unnecessarily also contributes to the perception SWAT is a standoffish, elite group whose members think they're better than their fellow officers. Any SWAT commander worth his/her salt should go out of the way to include non-SWAT personnel as integral to the success of an overall mission. Every responder is important, and every job — whether performed by a SWAT member or reserve officer — is critical to the success of the overall operation.

Not Political Tools

To avoid the potential for inappropriate use of the SWAT resource, enlightened teams use a matrix to determine if a SWAT response is justified. Such a matrix assigns a numerical value to each of a series of considerations regarding the incident. The points are tallied, and unless the minimum acceptable level is attained, SWAT isn't used.

And while it wasn't directly discussed in Balko's article, it was clearly implied: SWAT should not and cannot allow itself to become a tool of politicians, nor can it become a force in opposition to the Constitutional protections we enjoy as citizens. Accuse me of overreacting, but the potential for government administrations to commandeer and use SWAT to pursue inappropriate agendas is high. As the ones responsible for the execution of SWAT missions, our oath is to the Constitution, not those who happen to hold elective office at any particular point in time. We need to guard against such potential misuse at all costs.

In the past, many agencies have financed much of our specialized SWAT equipment — weapons, hard armor, robots, NVD's and vehicles — through federal grants. Read the fine print before you apply for your next grant of this type. Any requirement that said equipment be made available for federal use staffed by city, county or state level officers may well be in violation of both the Constitution and federal law. Consider this before jumping full steam ahead into competition for such grants.

Setting Realistic Expectations

The supervisor of a vice/narcotics unit from a medium-size municipal law enforcement agency asked me to address the issue of selecting personnel for specialty assignments. As he puts it, management is split between those who feel time in patrol should be the determining factor and those who believe additional preparation in addition to patrol experience is necessary.

Another reader is concerned about whether such assignments should be "forever" or of a fixed duration requiring officers to rotate to another assignment once the fixed duration has been met.

Nothing Is Forever

I firmly believe specialty assignments should not be "lifetime" assignments. Even those with a substantial learning curve should be of fixed duration because no matter how motivated we are in the beginning, most of us tend to stagnate in the same work situation after a period of time. When this occurs the individual and the department suffers. I need look only to one of my academy training officers to underscore my position that certain assignments like vice, narcotics and criminal intelligence units need to have relatively short assignment periods.

This officer was a poster boy for the department. A former Marine, he was as squared away as you could imagine. He had significant patrol experience and after serving as an academy "DI" for a number of years requested a transfer to narcotics and the transfer was granted. There wasn't a mandatory rotation period and after a few years he went over to the other side — succumbing to the temptation of big money the dope trade presents. He stole and sold dope, and he gave up the identities of other undercover cops to the bad guys. This former Marine was fired, prosecuted and sent to prison. There are many similar examples that have caused me to always put a limit on the time my officers can spend in such assignments.

Proving You're Interested

If traffic enforcement/accident investigation is a specialty assignment, I can see it requiring only patrol experience because most patrol personnel are involved in traffic enforcement and, at least to a small degree, accident investigation. But it would certainly show initiative and motivation if an applicant for a traffic slot had taken an accident reconstruction course or a traffic enforcement course at the local community college — on his/her own time.

Other specialty assignments may require more knowledge of a particular subject in order to be a strong candidate for selection. Using narcotics as an example, there are generally a host of courses available through community college channels that a serious applicant for a dope cop position could elect to take. In my book, the candidate who's done so ranks ahead of the applicant who hasn't, assuming both have enough street time in patrol to meet basic standards for consideration.

Within the departments I've run, I've found it helpful to put into writing several things regarding specialty assignments. One, list all specialty assignments within the department and list the duration of each assignment, as it will vary. For example, a detective position in property crimes might be for a 5-year period while a narcotics investigator might be just 3 years ... for the reasons previously stated. Next, the "desired qualifications" for each position are listed. The property crimes position might require 4 years of patrol experience, including assignment as a field training officer. Completion of an advanced report writing class, competent or above evaluations since date of employment and completion of an evidence class could all also be requirements.

With this approach, officers who desire a certain special assignment can know — in advance — how long the assignment will last if they're selected and what they can do to prepare for such an assignment. Then, when the opening occurs, the department must stick to its guns. Those who've acquired the desired qualifications should certainly be given preference over those who've simply done their time in patrol with little or no extra effort.

Predictable Results

This approach isn't perfect and the criteria used will vary from agency to agency. There should be some objective and specific selection criteria attached to each specialty assignment; it's far better than the "it's who you know" method or strictly seniority-based approach some still use today. If the expectations are realistic and known in advance, the outcome should be predictable. Those who've prepared and shown initiative can predict success at some point in the future. Those who've done nothing to meet the desired qualifications will have no legitimate cause for complaint when not selected.

A Profession? Or Entitlement Job? Part 1

I've received several requests to address the seeming growth of an entitlement mentality within law enforcement, which serves to the detriment of the profession as a whole. In fact, as one asserted, this sense of entitlement is almost diametrically opposed to the very definition of professionalism itself. Readers shared examples of what they perceive to be an "it's-all-about-me" perspective on the part of some of our fellow officers. One cited the all too common expectation that after 2 or 3 years in patrol an officer is "entitled" to a specialty assignment … regardless of whether he or she has put any effort into preparing for it. Another cited the oft-stated belief: "if they expect me to train, they have to pay me for it."

While it's been longer ago than some of you have been alive, I vividly remember advice my FTO gave me many years ago. On our first night together in patrol he started the evening with orientation. After focusing on safety and equipment he said, "I have some advice for you, which you're free to accept or reject." His advice?

All the county owed me was basic safety equipment and a paycheck based upon the premise I worked 40 productive hours a week. Beyond that, what I did, the equipment I did it with, and what I would become over the course of my career was up to me. I could get by and likely "do my 30" in uniform, in patrol. By the way, there's nothing wrong with that, but it's important to understand it's a choice each individual officer makes.
More on that in a moment.

You're Owed Nothing

As examples of what he'd just said he pointed out the flashlight, holster and other issued equipment. They would "do the job," but there were better, safer and more effective equipment out there I might consider buying myself. He said, "the county doesn't have an obligation to provide you with everything you want. It's your choice, and if my life depended on it I would upgrade at my own expense." He had made that choice, as did I the very next day.

He went on to discuss several of our coworkers by name. Both had been in patrol for nearly 20 years. According to my FTO one of them chose patrol because he liked it. He was qualified for more than one specialty assignment and, in fact, had turned down transfers to detectives on multiple occasions. He was well respected and looked to as a mentor by many of us.

The other wasn't a longtime patrol officer by choice and couldn't understand why he hadn't been selected for a specialty assignment long ago. The cold hard fact was he'd done absolutely nothing to prepare for such an assignment and was only mediocre, at best, at patrol. His point of view was based solely on "time in grade;" he was entitled to get out of patrol, and because he hadn't he was disgruntled on his very best day.

Take Responsibility

What sets a profession apart from a job is the willingness of its practitioners to take personal responsibility for improving themselves. That can mean, at times, taking classes at personal expense, and devoting off-duty time to learning skill sets making you a serious contender for more glamorous assignments or for future promotion. Self-improvement and personal responsibility are qualities any sensible police manager or administrator will look for when selecting people for important assignments within the organization. If you believe you're entitled to something simply based on time spent in the organization, it's unlikely you'll achieve your goal. In short, you just don't get it.

While I'm not one to make excuses for the lazy or unmotivated, I do understand the causation of the entitlement mentality in our society today. It begins in childhood, is reinforced through much of our educational system, and is double reinforced by a political philosophy and government, which is determined to make people dependent at all costs. The "system" rewards those who feel entitled, often to the economic (and other) detriment of those who work hard to improve themselves.

It's not just our profession that suffers from this malady; it's almost epidemic in our nation today. The long-term costs of this orientation, however, are great. In the case of law enforcement, if entitlement becomes both the expectation and the reality, any thought of maintaining police work as a profession rather than simply a job will be lost. We'll continue to address this topic next month.

A Profession? Or Entitlement Job? Part 2

Last month, we discussed the entitlement mentality within our profession. Now I'd like to explore the issue further, as I believe it's critical to the question of whether we remain a profession or revert to a time when police work was simply a job almost anyone could do.

One of those who originally suggested this topic opined that the entitlement mentality plaguing too many police agencies is the logical outgrowth of the union or organized labor orientation of many of today's cops. While that view may be controversial, I happen to think it's true. Consider the following, because if you're honest and have been around long enough, you'll recognize this scenario to be true.

Once Upon A Time...

Some years back, an officer suggested to the chief of a neighboring police department the benefits of adding a patrol canine to the force. If the department would assist in funding the dog he, the officer, would volunteer to be the handler and would attend the training on his own time. The city, of course, would also need to provide a suitable vehicle, but the officer would purchase other requisite equipment himself and would happily house the dog at his home during off-duty hours.

The administration viewed the proposal positively, as it allowed them (or so they thought) to add a beneficial resource in a relatively cost-effective manner. From the officer's point of view, though he never said so, he just created a prestigious specialty assignment tailor-made for him. So the deal was done. And, yes, the department and the community benefitted from the K-9 in patrol program over a period of several years.

Three years down the road, the "police association" (a politically correct term for "union") decided that in spite of the handler initiating the K-9 program and practically begging to be allowed to donate some of the costs, a huge inequity had occurred. Said association, in the form of a grievance and threatened lawsuit, demanded the handler be reimbursed for all he'd spent in support of the dog, compensated for a ridiculous amount of time allegedly spent working the dog at home off-duty, and compensation for portal-to-portal travel time. The association held the officer was "entitled" to such compensation. I'll spare the details but the city paid big and that was the end of the K-9 program.

Noseless Faces

Further, many departments, even in this period of ammunition shortages and excessive costs, still allocate practice ammo monthly to their officers as an incentive to maintain and improve life-saving skills. Unfortunately, too many officers and the associations representing them eschew this benefit and exclaim, "We won't train if we're not paid." Ever heard the expression, "Don't cut your nose off to spite your face?"

A true professional devotes whatever time, talent and even treasure as reasonable and necessary to maintain and even improve his skills. Someone who simply holds a job does only what he's paid for and uses only those resources provided to him at the company's expense to maintain minimum levels of competency. You'd think that in a line of work where your life, the life of a fellow officer or the lives of citizens might depend on the maximum proficiency attainable by you, an offer of practice ammo at no cost would be well-received. But in an entitlement society? Not so much.

Think About It

The truly professional peace officer takes what is given by the agency, and through personal initiative — on his own time — uses what's given to him as a foundation upon which to build. Those who do not add value (their own efforts) to the mix never get beyond the foundation itself. Reading job-related materials or participating in self-funded training during off-duty hours is a good investment in your future. Professionals do it all the time. Mere holders of jobs never do it at all.

The future of law enforcement, and whether it remains a profession or reverts to the blue-collar job level it once was, is up to each and every one of us. For those of us who desire to remain professional and skilled, please give us all the free ammo you can afford — we'll use it productively on our own time to better prepare ourselves to go home safe at the end of each shift.

The entitlement folks? They'll put their trust in luck, not in personal responsibility and initiative. I know which side I'm on. Do you?

We Are Not Doing Ourselves Any Favors

Other columns in the *From the Chief* series have addressed the issue of police militarization. While I am and will always be a firm supporter of law enforcement having all of the tools needed to get the job done, to protect the public, and to protect themselves, there is a key point that it appears is being increasingly ignored. That point is that it is of paramount importance to use *only* those tools needed to safely complete a given mission and no more. I have made the point that using a rock crusher when a small hammer alone will get the job done is not in our best interests. While we cannot let the publics' or the politicians' perception of what we do and how we do it interfere with our ability to function professionally there is no question that perceptions can negatively impact law enforcement. Negative perceptions, particularly when we have the ability to prevent them, will only harm us and tie our hands in the long run.

There was recently an officer involved shooting (OIS) in Ferguson, MO which has aroused much public and political attention. Not surprising the current occupier of the White House, whom I not so affectionately refer to as the mouth who roars, entered into the fray. As usual he comments were based upon bias rather than fact. Interestingly, however, some politicians of note who are generally regarded as conservatives and staunch supporters of the police also offered negative comments about the way the post shooting riots were handled by local law enforcement. The basis of their criticism was not whether law enforcement should have quelled the riots but on the tools law enforcement chose to use to do so. This incident, and there are other examples like it, re-directed the discussion to the "militarization of the police". So volatile was this incident's aftermath that bills were introduced to prohibit the much needed distribution of excess military equipment to civilian law enforcement. That is not a good thing and it was and is preventable.

There's That "Militarization" Thing Again

The facts regarding the Ferguson shooting, and whether it was justified, will be determined not in the court of public or political opinion but by the very justice system which has worked effectively in the United States since its founding. Frankly whether it was a "good shoot" or not has become somewhat of a secondary issue. The fact is, as is so often the case, that the shooting was used as an excuse for law violators to engage in destructive criminal acts. As we have seen in Los Angeles, Detroit, and many other places "protest" was used as justification (there is no justification) for looting and burning. If my experience in responding to many riots in Los Angeles earlier in my career is any indicator most of the rioters have no idea what the facts are regarding the OIS and, frankly they most likely don't care. The incident simply provided cover for them to take what was not theirs and destroy what were likely the only businesses of their type catering to that particular small town.

Use the Tools Necessary

Clearly law enforcement has a responsibility to respond to and quell riots. And, they have an obligation to use assets which minimize the risk to themselves, the general public, and even those engaged in rioting. I've participated in multiple riot responses in an era before Lenco Bearcats™ and MRAPS had even been developed. The tactics for riot dispersal involved personnel using formations and non lethal weapons effectively. Vehicles were only of value to get us to and from the riot scene.

We are now in a different era where equipment designed for one purpose (SWAT type incidents) is being used almost routinely if for no other reason than the intimidation factor. That is, in my view, a misguided approach since it creates an impression and an environment that leaves us wide open to a charge of "militarization". If during the course of a riot a barricaded situation evolves then, yes, bring in the heavy artillery, MRAP or otherwise. But the Ferguson riots didn't involve that. It was, according to police sources who were on scene, a matter of trained officers using chemical agents and other less than lethal devices to disperse and discourage those who would loot and burn. The presence of intimidating equipment such as APC's of both civilian and military derivation served only to reinforce the perception that local law enforcement viewed themselves as military like occupation forces.

The risks to an overuse of important equipment when and where it is not actually needed are that we will by legislative mandate suffer the loss of those resources altogether. That may be one of the outcomes of Ferguson and, if that happens, it will be a sad day for law enforcement—particularly since that reaction could have been prevented.

Political Correctness and the Federal Government

News today is that the federal government, in its infinite wisdom (not!) is suing the Pennsylvania State Police in order to require them to establish different physical fitness standards for female recruits as opposed to male recruits. This is but the latest in a string of efforts on the part of the feds to dictate to state and local governments. On the one hand, the federal government often through the Department of Justice (which under the present regime is clearly a misnomer) preaches the need for "equality" and forces it down our throats…then, on the other hand they pursue courses of action designed to insure that things are anything but equal.

If I were a female recruit I would be incensed at what the federal government is attempting to impose. My goal would be to become a thoroughly qualified, professional peace officer every bit equal to my peers regardless of gender. If I were a female recruit with some knowledge of the real world of the streets I would be more than just a little incensed. I would be outraged that the federal government is perfectly OK putting me on the streets, with all of the risks to my health and safety involved, with a lesser level of training than my male counterparts. Talk about discrimination! When it comes to my safety I would want no "shortcuts" in my preparation, and no allowing me to succeed in a profession where my very survival , and the safety of the public I serve, might depend upon my ability to mix it up with the best of them.

Standards Must Be Equal

Relaxing physical fitness standards serves no one's best interests. I worked with, and helped train, some of the very first female patrol officers in the United States back in the 1960's and 70's. They worked under some severe handicaps, none of their making. The faced true discrimination by male cops who believed that having a

woman as a partner was an officer safety risk. The ladies proved
them wrong. They were at a disadvantage in terms of uniforms and
equipment that was inferior to and less practical than that issued to
their male partners. Those issues, too, were overcome in time. The
one thing, however, that those female officer pioneers that I worked
with did not have to overcome was the perception (much less the
reality) that they were held to a lower physical fitness standard than
male officers. The reason? Because they were not. Same standard,
same performance requirement and for reasons the "PC" federal
government simply cannot seem to get through their thick heads---
because all cops, male or female, 5 feet tall or 6 feet 5 face the same
risks. Those risks may not be capable of resolution by physical
fitness. That's why we have weapons of various types issued to us.
If, however, defensive tactics, which require physical fitness can
resolve a particular conflict it is inexcusable to not require all
officers to meet the same physical fitness standard.

The "Feds" Are Not a Good Example

In my opinion the feds would do well to butt out of the training of
cops. If the performance of some federal law enforcement personnel
is any indicator, police training is not something the feds are
particularly expert at. If someone (male or female) is being denied
an opportunity in this profession based solely on sex, that's one
thing. If they fail because they cannot perform physically at a level
which could save their life or someone else's, that's another.

Let's Be Honest About It

As this is being written the United States Department of Justice has just chastised one of the nation's largest municipal law enforcement agencies for intentional mis-reporting (under reporting) of criminal activity in its jurisdiction. Knowing that agency, and having colleagues whom I know that work for it, this is not the first time that department has engaged in such behavior. It is simply the first time they have been caught at it.

Exactly what has the agency done that has aroused the ire of the feds? In the instant case they downgraded serious, violent, felony assaults to less serious misdemeanors and reported them as such. One might wonder why an agency would do that. Simple. If you as the Chief, or if the department as a whole, wants to make it appear that your crime fighting efforts against violent offenses is effective you have to show a reduction in the number of such acts reported to police. There are a couple of ways of doing that, one involving aggressive policing and the other by simply "cooking the books".

The Right Way to Reduce Crime

Aggressive policing within the law and using Constitutionally permitted tactics and techniques is the correct way of addressing crime problems. But that takes work and commitment and is often not well received by liberal elements within the community who decry any tough enforcement measures as discriminatory and oppressive. So, if the objective is to make the department look good without inviting an outcry from some elements within the community it is all too tempting to just "re-classify" some (in this cases thousands) of instances of felonious behavior.

It should be noted for the record that this practice within that particular agency became accepted, and some would say encouraged, upon the arrival of a new chief of police. That chief, according to reliable sources, had used the same tactic in his prior (very large) agency. In fact, he was selected as chief of the department slammed by the feds because he was thought to possess some magic ability to reduce serious crime. What in fact he was good at was "massaging" numbers to make himself look good—something he has built a career on.

Speak the Truth

It was once the prevailing, professional position among police leaders that if nothing else we owed the public the truth. If community support for crime reduction (which is as much a public responsibility as a police responsibility) was to exist it needed to be founded on an accurate picture of just what the extent of crime actually was. For them to get that picture it needs to be painted in honesty, not painted by false manipulation of facts.

There are a number of downsides to under-reporting crime. In the instant case it was downgrading felony assaults to the misdemeanor level. That agency, and others, have marched down the same road by downgrading burglaries (or B &E—felonies) to misdemeanor trespass violations. The downsides are: #1, the public has been lied to which, when that fact is discovered, does nothing more than erode public confidence and trust in the police; #2 it deprives the agency of what might be much needed resources. If serious, indeed violent, crime is increasing perhaps more officers are needed. If declining, appropriate staffing levels will not be granted—in fact they may be reduced; #3. It is unjust and unfair to crime victims. Violent assaults should, and usually do, receive a follow up investigation by detectives. If the incident is mis-classified as a misdemeanor that follow up will likely not occur to the detriment of the victim. And, often, those victims are members of minority communities whose distrust of the police will only be exacerbated by the false reporting of incidents in which they were victimized.

Regrettably while it was one big city police department that got caught in the act of false reporting it is a trend that is not that uncommon. Too many so-called police leaders today put political correctness and/or their own personal interests ahead of their responsibility to be honest with the people they serve. Unfortunately, given the tenor of our times, it is a trend not likely to be reversed anytime soon unless those perpetrating such frauds suffer some significant consequences for their dishonesty.

If Good Leaders Don't Speak Up, We Are Screwed

There was a time in the history of our profession when politicians and the public listened to what law enforcement leaders had to say instead of dictating to law enforcement as happens so often today. Of course, that was at a time when most Police Chiefs and Sheriffs were of like mind that their role was to protect and serve the public in ways that most effectively combated crime. Politics and political considerations seldom if ever dissuaded an ethical chief from telling it like it was. There was even a time when the only organization that represented police chiefs was committed to telling the truth even when the truth was unpopular and not something elected officials wanted to hear.

The days I have just described are long gone. The largest organization which now represents police chiefs long ago bowed to political correctness and is a lap dog for those who advocate extreme gun control measures, legalization of marijuana and a host of other things which **real** cops know are just so much political BS. Fortunately, the national organization which represents Sheriffs seems cut from a different cloth and has not yet yielded to the whims of liberal politicians.

Autonomy is Needed

Effective law enforcement requires a certain degree of autonomy. Chiefs must be able, without political interference, to tailor police services to fit the needs of individual communities. What works (or, more honestly what doesn't work) in Chicago may not have any application at all in Spokane. Yet, with increasing regularity, we see Chiefs trying to emulate agencies which have gained political popularity even at the expense of jeopardizing local public safety and at the expense of tossing out the very Constitution we are sworn to uphold and protect.

As a profession we are about to suffer the loss of our ability to self-regulate and self-determine. We are, by sucking up to elected officials whose motives are suspect and whom we should not trust, allowing them to dictate for us what is acceptable police practice, what weapons are "acceptable", and what tactics we must use when suppressing riots or engaging in other dangerous activities. And we have only ourselves to blame for that. How?

Individual Responsibility is Critical

We have yielded to a national organization, and in many states to state police chief organizations, the right to speak for us as individuals regarding which politicians and which proposed laws to endorse. Bad move. The outcome of that is, with police endorsements, the election of Governors, Attorney Generals, and members of Congress who are at best closet opponents of effective police work. The outcome of that is the passage of legislation allowing for the legalization of marijuana and the granting of drivers licenses to persons who are not legally in this country---both bad, but becoming law nevertheless.

Chiefs without ethics or whose sole focus is narcissistic are more than willing to let others speak for them as long as, in their view, it makes them look good.   Others, who put professionalism ahead of self-centeredness speak out individually when their conscience mandates that they do so. They also avoid the "mainstream" police organizations which they know do not represent the best interests of law enforcement or the public. Instead, they are active participants in organizations such as (in the region applicable) the Border Sheriffs Association or the Constitutional Sheriffs and Peace Officers Association.

I'm sure there are some readers who believe with all their hearts that I am a conspiracy theorist and am "out there" in some right wing fringe group. Actually I'm neither, but I do pride myself on being observant regarding what is happening in this country. I can also add, without "Common Core" thank you, 2 plus 2 and arrive at 4 as the correct answer. What is happening to our profession in terms of emasculating its leadership is exactly what has happened to the military over the past six years. Good leaders in both professions, are being purged and replaced with yes men…and yes men by their behavior have proven to be unethical and capable of not only bad law enforcement but intentional law violations. And that I find to be very, very scary.

Have We "Lost" the Oath of Office?

It has been my privilege, over a period of many decades, to serve as a member of six different law enforcement agencies in several states. Each time I moved from one agency to another I was required to repeat the oath of office attendant to the position of peace officer. It was my honor to do so. An oath, by definition, is a solemn promise to do something. In the case of a peace officer it is swearing to uphold the Constitution of the United States of America and the Constitution of the state in which we are employed. It is a promise to uphold the laws which we are empowered to enforce.

Based upon our system of government almost all elected officials, and certainly our highest elected officials such as the President of the United States and the Governors of our fifty States, take an oath at the time they assume the duties of their office. In the case of the President, the oath includes defending the nation's Constitution. The oath taken by most Governors is to uphold the Constitution of the State and to enforce its laws. Given the widespread, and apparently growing, tendency for some of our elected officials to ignore--- actually, make that violate—their oath of office one must wonder if, as a nation we have "lost" the Oath of Office. Because cops take oaths similar to elected officials, and because some in law enforcement violate that oath, one must wonder if oaths in general have been "lost".

Oaths Are Not Ignored by Accident

I am of the firm belief that one does not "loose" an oath of office. If an oath is violated, or ignored, it is by choice. A "loss" can be accidental. What is happening in this country today, in too many places involving too many people, is no accident. It is a conscious and, in my opinion, treasonous choice engaged in by people who believe our nation's system of government and laws do not apply to them.

Let's look at some examples. The current occupier of the White House has chosen to ignore, and have his minions ignore, a whole host of laws. Examples are almost too numerous to mention but we can begin with the Defense of Marriage Act, and move on from there to laws pertaining to illegal entry into the United States and the use of a substance (marijuana) that is still illegal under federal law.

At least two Governors (Oregon and Washington) have openly stated that during their reign the death penalty (which is the LAW in both states as a result of a vote of the people) will not be enforced. Who gave them the power, I wonder, to function not only as executives but as legislators? I guess, as at the federal level, separation of powers no longer applies to (some) states either.

You may wonder why, in a column devoted to law enforcement officers, I raise the subject of oaths. Glad you asked. It is our oath of office---that is our solemn promise—that separates us from the vast majority of government workers. In fact, it is that oath which separates us from the majority of people period. It is that oath which has, throughout our history as a profession, always made us special. It is not just the fact that we are the nation's wolf hunters, warriors and sheepdogs by choice. It is because we have sworn to perform that function no matter what the challenge, no matter what the risk, and no matter what the consequence. Cops run *to* the sound of gunfire out of both internal motivation and obligation. That obligation comes, in part, from the fact that we swore to do whatever needs done to uphold the laws of the particular jurisdiction in which we practice our profession.

Have we "lost" the oath of office in law enforcement much as it has been lost at other levels of government? My contact with cops on the street says not only NO, but hell no. At so called leadership levels, particularly in some larger policing agencies, the hell no seems not to apply....and that concerns me. When "top cops" choose to ignore some duly enacted laws because "someone might be offended" they have bailed on the oath they took to enforce all laws entrusted to their care. When that happens, as seems to be occurring in too many of our country's largest cities and counties, that is plain dangerous. It tells the public that if they protest loud enough certain "unpopular" laws may no longer be enforced. It serves as an excuse for other, heretofore principled, agencies to slide into the same abyss. It demoralizes those cops who took their oath seriously. And, in the long run, it destroys the integrity of the profession as a whole.

We Need to be Very Watchful

The late and great gunslinger Col. Jeff Cooper is credited with developing the system of situational awareness that cops use to insure their safety. I've been living in "Condition Yellow" for most of my working life with occasional forays into "Orange" and even "Red". Well folks I honestly believe that in terms of the relationship of our oath of office to our standing as a profession we are at "Orange". If we do not guard against the growing disregard for our oath we are in for some very dangerous times. Just as we guard against threats to our person we must now guard against threats to that which makes us good, different, and valued---our oath of office. Please join with me in maintaining a heightened state of vigilance. We may be the last bastion of defense for our Nation's Constitution, separation of powers, and rule of law.

You Have to Be Kidding Me

By the time this column is printed, the fate of rogue ex-cop Christopher Dorner will most likely have been decided. I for one have my own thoughts on what should be the fate of one who, for any reason, targets law enforcement officers and, in the case of the Riverside, California officers, commits an outright assassination of them.

My purpose in addressing the Dorner crime spree has less to do with him than another peripheral but related issue. Dorner himself is not worth wasting print ink on. The related issue is the reaction of the current chief of his former department and how, once again, political correctness rather than doing the right thing drives the actions of some so-called police leaders today.

Shortly following Dorner's murder of a young couple, his murder of a police officer and the attempted murder of two other officers his "manifesto" was widely published in the media and was posted on line for all to read. In it, a lengthy and somewhat rambling piece, he justified his planned attacks on cops and their families because in his view he had been falsely terminated from his employing agency. Only the twisted mind of someone who should never have been a cop in the first place could justify killing officers he had never met, much less the family members of those officers. Then, rather than target only the agency against which he felt he had a "beef", he blows away officers on "routine patrol" miles away from his former jurisdiction while they were stopped for a red traffic control signal. That alone, in my view, should have dictated one and only one response from any police leader. And, that response should not have, in any way, even remotely implied that the assertions made by Dorner in his manifesto contained even a grain of truth.

The agency from which Dorner was terminated is not perfect. None are. But Dorner's firing went through a detailed, lengthy, and thorough appeals process. His termination was upheld after testimony and an opportunity for Dorner to present his defense. End of story. Well, not quite.

Appeasement is Often NOT the Right Thing to Do

Following Dorner's initial, brutal, calculated criminal rampage the current chief of his former department announced that they would take another look at the circumstances of Dorner's firing. In my view there is absolutely no, as in zilch, zero, nada, justification for doing so other than appeasement. Appeasement most often has little to do with the truth and is designed solely to deflect criticism and, usually, to deflect criticism from the person doing the appeasing. In other words, the chief was covering his butt and in a sense threw his department, and its former leadership, under the bus in the process. There is a word for that---actually two. One is cowardly, the other despicable.

But, but, but, some have argued a "reopening" of Dorner's termination case might cause him to cease his assaults on LEO's. It might even motivate him to surrender. Give me a break! The guy, at the time the "re-investigation" was announced, was the suspect in three murders and two attempted murders of law enforcement officers. He was flat out a death penalty candidate. Anyone who seriously believed that "appeasement" would cause Dorner to change his well thought out plans needs a blood test. I'd really like to know what sort of dope they were using to even suggest Dorner "might" surrender.

The "appeasement" effort which occurred in this case is unique and, in my opinion, extreme. But appeasement and the political correctness that underlies it is becoming all too common in our profession. The examples leaders set roll down hill in any department. Good examples live forever in the careers of young and impressionable officers. So do bad examples. The example given in this case was anything but good.

Mandatory Retirement?

In his Return Fire letter in the March 2014 issue retired Lieutenant John Lane asked a number of provocative questions. One of them was "Are you in favor of straight 20 year retirement and mandatory retirement?" Not that I speak officially for the Publisher/Editor of American Cop, but I'll take a stab at answering that particular query.

My answer is "yes and no". How is that for sitting on top of the fence, something that those who know me and follow my columns seldom see me do. I say yes and no for the following reasons. One, I believe that a straight 20 year retirement should be an option for those who want it and can afford it. I do not, however, believe the net financial benefit to a 20 year retiree should equal that of someone who has devoted 30 years to the profession. Fortunately most retirement systems with which I am familiar would not allow that to happen. The retirement formula is generally "X" percent of salary times the number of years of service. If, at say 3%, a 20 year veteran can afford to retire (his retirement using the aforementioned formula would be 60% of his final salary while employed) good for him or her IF that is what the employee elects to do.

Are You Fit?

The above approach certainly opens the door for a lot of folks beginning a second career if they choose to and at a very young age—perhaps 41 or 42. I would not, however, advocate that someone be forced to retire after a straight 20 years of service. There are too many cops who in their early 40's are still physically and psychologically fit and still highly motivated to serve. There are legions of examples of cops serving productively into their 60's, enough of them to argue effectively against mandatory retirement at an earlier age.

There is a downside to the straight 20 and out approach. Actually, there are several downsides that occur to me. One is the loss to the department of experienced, trained, and highly valuable human resources and the cost to the agency of training replacements. The second downside that I see is a real lack of qualified personnel to fill the top leadership positions on any department. Think about that using the following hypothetical example.

Jane Jones enters law enforcement on her 21st birthday. She joins a department that mandates the 20 year retirement Lieutenant Lane alludes to. She spends 4 months in the academy and another 4 months in the FTO program. By the time she becomes a confident, self-motivated, competent street cop over a year has passed. She elects to spend a total of 4 years in patrol to hone her basic police skills and then, successfully, applies for the first of several specialty assignments. Special assignment number one is traffic accident investigation and she serves in that capacity for 3 years. She then takes the investigative experience she has gained and applies for a position as property crimes investigator. She serves 3 years in that assignment before seeking a promotion to Sergeant. Already one half of her allotted 20 years is behind her.

She promotes to Sergeant and after a relatively short (3 year) tenure at that rank she applies for Lieutenant and one year after testing she receives the bar on her collar. She has six years left before she is shown the door under mandatory retirement. Perhaps she is a solid mid manager (Lieutenant) after 4 years at that rank, and assuming there is a Captain's position that might come open, she would be a viable candidate. But would the agency be well-served by promoting someone to Captain's rank who could not serve more than two years? I doubt it. Left out of the equation is the issue of who, in 20 years, might ever gain the knowledge, experience, and other qualifications needed to rise to the office of Chief? And, if some miracle cop could, how long would s/he have left to serve as top cop with the 20 year service cap? Not much I'm afraid.

So while I support a retirement system which allows (optional) a 20-year retirement for those who can afford it, I absolutely oppose such a short term career being mandatory. If such a mandatory system were implemented, we would quickly, I believe, come to regret it. Rather than experience at the top of the organization and the sound decision making which should come with experience, we would have something entirely different. What we would have is what is sometimes referred to as the "boy wonder" (or girl, for that matter): one who rapidly rises through the ranks based upon textbook knowledge, but with little real world lumps-and-bumps experience. Goodness knows we already have enough of that type. No reason to invite the problem to get worse.

Do We Really Want to Go There?

Like many American Cop readers I watched with interest, and frankly some dismay, as the Bureau of Land Management (BLM) recently attempted to enforce a court order on the Bundy Ranch in Clark County Nevada. Make no mistake about two things: one, while I believe in the United States Constitution and have more than once taken an oath to uphold and defend it, I am not what is currently referred to as a "Constitutionalist"; two, I understand the rule of law and whether one agrees or not there was, at the time of this incident, a court order in effect giving BLM legal authority to enforce its provisions.

It's Not the *What,* But the *How*

My concern has much less to do with *what* BLM was legally empowered to do than with the *how.* In an era when there is growing distrust of the federal government and an increasing concern about law enforcement becoming too militarized the handling of Bundy Ranch did absolutely nothing to quell those concerns. In fact, the show and use of force accomplished just the opposite.

Law enforcement officials have a multitude of responsibilities. One of those is to handle incidents, particularly those likely to engender widespread media attention, in a manner that showcases professionalism and sensitivity to public concerns. Certainly if the use of force is anticipated we have every right and responsibility to be prepared for that. However, an excessive show of force on the "front lines" at the outset of an incident can invite something which might not otherwise have occurred absent that show of force.

Don't Invite Trouble

I wasn't there, but I know some people who were and their credentials for objectivity and honesty are impeccable. Given their law enforcement backgrounds I trust, also, in their ability to gather, analyze and act based on good intelligence information. Their assessment was, being there "on the ground", that at the outset neither the Bundys nor anyone else posed a threat that justified the front line display of BLM K-9 units, snipers, APC's or most of the other heavy hardware BLM deployed from the beginning. Yes, after the Bundy's situation became well known there was an influx of supporters from across the country and some of them were (lawfully) armed members of the "militia". One must wonder if, absent BLM's overt display of weaponry, those folks would have traveled to Clark County in the first place.

As a professional LEO there are several related issues which concern me as well. The first is why BLM even has some of the assets that were on display at Bundy Ranch. The BLM's purpose and the **limited** law enforcement authority they are granted under federal law, is to serve as the guardians of public lands under their jurisdiction. Are K-9 units, SWAT Teams, and APC's really needed consistent with that mission? In the very rare instance where such assets might be needed (and I am not at all convinced they were at Bundy Ranch) could not such resources be provided by other federal agencies (like the FBI) which actually have a real need for them? That leads to my second concern.

I've spent my career in county and municipal law enforcement and I understand both the concept and practical aspects of "mutual aid". However, in any jurisdiction I have ever worked mutual aid is neither automatic nor is it guaranteed. An agency which is requested to respond generally can decline to do so and does not need to give a reason. Nobody asked me but if I were in charge of decision making at Las Vegas Metro I would have declined BLM's invitation to provide an APC and SWAT resources to the Bundy Ranch incident. Unless my aged eyes are failing me the videos I saw captured a SWAT APC on scene conspicuously marked with that agency's identifier .

A Better Use

While I don't take credit for raising the following issue I certainly agree with the question. If BLM has such a large number of specialized resources why is it that the one and only time they have displayed them is in enforcing a court order against a single family? Having worked much of my career in very close proximity to the US-Mexican border I know that there are hundreds of thousands of acres of BLM land adjacent to that border. That large expanse of U S land has been decimated by the daily travel of thousands of illegal immigrants, including drug cartel runners. Damage to that land is far, far worse than several hundred head of cattle could ever inflict. If BLM is really itching to show off and justify its collection of military-like assets maybe their ground adjacent to the border is the place to do it. Deterring illegal immigration through a show of force seems far more productive and constitutionally correct than driving out of business a ranch that existed long before BLM and its "rules" were ever created.

Favoritism: The Cancer That Kills

There are a lot of things that can adversely impact morale within a police organization. Understaffing which results in excessive amounts of forced overtime is one. Inadequate equipment is another. A third is a lack of or poor training. Poor supervision must be included as well. In my experience, however, there is one activity which, particularly when it occurs at the top of the organization, is the most damaging to morale and good order within the department. That is when the chief him/her self plays favorites.

Many law enforcement agencies are part of a larger government entity that has in place some sort of civil service system or personnel system which seeks to insure that certain steps are followed in the hiring and promotional processes. This, among other reasons, is to minimize the chances of favoritism entering into personnel decisions. No system, however, is perfect and anyone astute enough to have been appointed chief of police is astute enough to find ways around the personnel/civil service system that is in place.

Impressions Are Important

What are some examples of this favoritism of which I speak. One is giving one candidate preferential treatment in the hiring process while finding a way to exclude others from the competition. Convincing the civil service commission or personnel officer to restrict the hiring for a police officer position to "in house" candidates only is one way of doing that. Don't get me wrong, there are times when that approach is appropriate. Restricting police officer hiring to the department's corps of Reserve Officers can have lots of advantages---assuming that there are multiple Reserves eligible to compete. Restricting a police officer hiring process to "non-sworn" employees when, in fact, there is only one non-sworn employee at the very least gives rise to the impression of favoritism having been shown.

Pre-selecting a hire from a pool of one as just described is only made worse when portion(s) of the normal and customary testing process are waived. If the normal process includes interview, written, physical agility, psychological evaluation, and background investigation all of those elements need to be included for every hire or, again, at the very least the impression that favoritism has occurred will arise among the troops. And, the effect of that will not be good.

When an employee of any particular job classification seems, from an objective view, to always get preferential treatment when it comes to assignments, shifts and work schedule again it gives rise to at least the perception that favoritism is occurring. A professional chief will insure that this does not happen. All members of a particular job classification should have equal opportunity with outcomes based upon such factors as enumerated in civil service or personnel rules….and nothing else. Seniority and merit may be two of those factors depending on the agency. The personal likes and relationships between the chief and an individual employee should never be part of the equation.

Anyone who has worked in a cop shop for any length of time can, undoubtedly, provide a list of examples of what the troops see as favoritism so rather than provide more examples let's talk about the negative impacts when real or perceived favoritism exists. The negative impact on morale, alluded to previously, is not to be scoffed at. Most cops won't argue with the notion that success within the organization should depend on performance of job related duties. When they perceive, based upon objective observation, that someone has the inside track due to a relationship and not due to job performance it rubs them raw. It is a de-motivator which can easily lead to the conclusion that no matter how hard I work I won't reap the benefits. It is particularly demoralizing when the "favorite" employee reaps benefits in spite of lacking competence in the duties which s/he is assigned.

When the "favorite" is the opposite sex of the chief a whole new world of assumption possibilities is opened up. Whether true or not, the "favorite status" will be attributed to an inappropriate, perhaps sexual, relationship between the chief and subordinate. To do anything which gives rise to such an attribution is not in the best interests of the chief or employee, nor is it professional.

So what's the cure? Just prior to being promoted to Sergeant many years ago, I was sent to a "supervisors' school" to learn all I would ever need to know as a supervisor. Well, the school fell short of that objective but one thing I did learn which served me well over my career was this. A supervisor (manager, executive) cannot be effective if s/he has too close of a personal relationship with any employee under his/her command. Supervisors should be friendly towards but not friends with people whom they supervise on the job as long as they are that person's supervisor. All employees supervised should be treated the same in terms of personal relationships and the higher one goes in the organization, rank wise, the more true that is.

Let me conclude by saying that in each organization I have led, I have had my favorites. They were my favorites because of their work ethic and performance. But neither they nor any other employee ever knew who my favorites were. It's just better that way.

Political Correctness: Throwing the truth and the troops under the bus

There was a time in this profession when the leaders of police organizations understood that in addition to responsibility and accountability to the public they also had responsibilities to the troops that served under them. Having worked for police leaders who understood that responsibility and took it seriously was, to say the least, a positive motivator especially in terms of morale.

When an accusation was made against an officer a good police leader would conduct a thorough investigation. If that investigation warranted further action such as a referral to the prosecutor or taking a case to the Grand Jury that is exactly what would happen. Everyone knew that, and they accepted it.

If the investigation revealed that the officer had done no wrong or if the matter was pending review by one of the aforementioned entities the police chief would, at worst, take a neutral position. If the matter was pending no responsible, conscientious, professional chief would take a public position which could in any manner imply wrongdoing on the part of the officer. If the investigation was complete and the officer(s) exonerated the chief would publicly defend them and explain the reasons why.

Implications Hurt

Well, in too many places today that once honored approach seems to no longer exist. Chief after Chief, in public statements following perhaps controversial incidents, adopt the politically correct position and in the process at least by implication the involved officers are thrown under the bus.

At the time of this writing the City of Ferguson, Missouri is still dealing with the aftermath of an incident in which one of its police officers shot an adult to death following a confrontation in the street.

The fact is, perhaps unknown to the involved officer, that the suspect had just committed a strong armed robbery at a nearby convenience store. The fact is that the suspect was a very large individual, much larger physically than the officer. The fact is that in the course of the confrontation, prior to the officer employing deadly force, the officer was injured and rather severely at that. The fact is that the officer did shoot and kill the suspect.

What is not clear, even at this writing, is whether the use of deadly force was necessary and justified. It is very clear that political pressure from a number of levels of government, including a president of the United States who should learn to keep his mouth shut, is condemning the officer in the media and court of public opinion. This is being done even though there is conflicting evidence, conflicting witnesses, and in spite of the fact that the case has yet to be brought before the Grand Jury.

There have been calls for the Chief of Police to resign. His response has been, quite frankly, both disgusting and disappointing. It is, in my opinion, a classic example of the dereliction of duty too common among today's top cops. Apparently, to save his job, he has "apologized" to the community for the manner in which this case was handled by his department. It does not take a rocket scientist to figure out that any apology prior to a resolution of the "shoot" issue by the Grand Jury will be construed as an admission that the Officer was wrong in his use of force. Talk about throwing one of the troops under the bus!

Nobody ever said the job of police chief will always be a bed of roses. The "honeymoon period" for a new chief, if there s one at all, lasts maybe six months. The duty of a chief is to do the right thing. It is not the duty of a chief to say or do whatever it takes to save his job, especially if to do so creates unwarranted problems for a subordinate. "Old school" chiefs seemed to have known that, perhaps intuitively. Many of today's chiefs don't seem to know that at all....and that, my friends, is to the detriment of the profession.

More Political Correctness

I recently read of an agency which has actually re-designed their uniform patch specifically for womens breast cancer awareness month. Now don't get me wrong, I have donated to cancer prevention but that was my money not the department's. The boastful account of the agency in question is that the special patch (with some of the patch's features in bright pink) will be worn by all personnel during breast cancer awareness month.

It occurs to me that those special patches weren't free nor is the task of changing out the patches (twice) without cost either. It may make the Chief and the department "look good" to some people but is that really a justified expenditure of the taxpayer's dollar?

Then there is the department which found it important to have some of its personnel march as an entry in a gay pride parade. Gays, last time I checked, represent about 3% of the population---a very vocal and politically active (in some places) 3%, but 3% nevertheless. Were those officers on duty anyhow, or were they brought in on overtime to participate? Of even greater importance, were any of them made to participate even if their particular religious beliefs do not support homosexuality?

Yes, as a profession we serve all people and do not discriminate on any grounds including sexual orientation. If the parade required a police presence for traffic or crowd control or some other reason of course officers should be assigned. That constitutes protection which is a perfectly legitimate function of our profession.

Was such participation as an active entry in the parade "protection" or was it pandering to one (small) element of the community? If it was pandering, I view that as just plain wrong. Participation in other than a peace/order keeping role (by marching as an element in the parade)implies endorsement. How and why can a police agency feel justified in endorsing 3% of the population at the expense of the other 97?

What Should We Be Training For?

There have been many accounts, in law enforcement media and elsewhere, of officer involved shootings in which an almost unbelievable number of rounds were fired by officers and in several of those instances, unfortunately, an innocent party was injured or killed by errant police rounds. Certainly there are times, and the North Hollywood Bank of America robbery/shootout is just one that comes to mind, when massive firepower is both necessary and justified. At times suppressive fire is needed to keep suspect(s) pinned down. At other times the structure or confines in which the suspect(s) are secreted warrant significant amounts of bullets going down range. But those are exceptions, not the rule.

The exceptions don't bother me. Instances where there is no exception yet an extreme number of rounds are fired do bother me More than bother me they have caused me to think why such "overkill" happens, and of greatest importance, what we can do to minimize such instances which are both dangerous to the public and fodder for incessant media criticism of law enforcement. My experience as a range instructor, SWAT operator, and SWAT commander tell me that the cause and the solution both rest in training.

When I entered this profession in the 1960's the department within which I cut my teeth in the business required firearms qualification every other month. Today required range training on that frequent a basis is seldom seen. The cost of ammunition and the cost of paying officers to participate are most often used as excuses for less frequent training. It is the rare department that even requires quarterly range qualification with many mandating training only twice, or in some cases even once, a year. It is not just the infrequency of training that is problematic but the content (or lack thereof) as well. While some agencies are able to provide realistic scenario based training which requires both tactical decision making and tactical movement in order to successfully complete the training evolution too many agencies still settle for putting round holes in paper targets at fixed distances with no stressors or movement involved. Therein, in my opinion, lies the problem.

What Training is Really Critical?

As street cops we are called upon to perform a lot of diverse tasks, some of which in my opinion we should not be engaged in. However, in this era of government pretending to be all things to all people at all times and lacking the fortitude to ever say "no" our brothers and sisters in blue get stuck performing all sorts of jobs that really shouldn't be ours in the first place. The fluffy, feel good things the politicians have us doing should, in fact, if done at all be done by someone else. What makes cops valuable is their willingness to perform those tasks no one else has the ability or stomach for. That includes the use of force, and sometimes the use of deadly force.

Since we are the only civilians in our society, other than executioners in prisons, empowered to take a human life we had damned well be good at it. Why? Because when such force is justified it needs to be decided on in a fraction of a second and executed expertly or the tragic collateral damage discussed in the first paragraph is more a probability than a possibility. Given that, it seems, at times, that our training priorities are screwed up to say the least.

We argue that we don't have money for ammunition or the training overtime necessary to insure weapons proficiency. Yet, too many police "leaders" have no problem making mandatory all manner of training in the feel good stuff that, frankly, a much lesser paid and lesser trained non-sworn employee could perform equally well. That, IMO, is a disservice to officers, to the department, and to the public we serve.

If we wish to employ force, particularly deadly force, expeditiously and accurately when it is necessary and justified we need to devote significant training to developing that skill set. We need such training to begin, not at the range, but in round table discussions designed to develop the ability to think tactically. To envision scenarios in which use of deadly force many not be just an option but the only option. To develop the ability to translate tactical thinking into tactical decision making of the highest order. And, then, to translate that into sound tactic movements employing our firearms in a manner that works against reflexive and inaccurate shooting. The day of justifying my putting lead downrange as a reflex response to the officer next to me firing his/her weapon is long gone. The decision to shoot must be an individual one based on specific facts and threats determined by me, not the officer next to me.

Unless and until we focus our training on what matters most none of what I have suggested will happen. The time to just "think about" the provision of such training is long past. It is time to do something about it.

CONCLUSION

At the end of each monthly *From the Chief* column in **AmericanCop** magazine I invited questions, comments and suggestions for future columns. One of the most enjoyable aspects of writing that column is that the Editor and I did get a lot of feedback and I received a lot of e-mails from people who just wanted to share an idea or get my take on an issue they were facing on their department. While I certainly do not pretend to have all the answers it was rewarding to at least be helpful.

AmericanCop in print is no more, so the opportunity for on line dialogue on a monthly basis no longer exists. However, I would be happy to exchange thoughts and ideas with readers of this book and can be contacted via exlasd@msn.com Take care, be safe, be honest, and be ethical

Jerry Boyd
Baker City, Oregon